KAREN SARGSYAN
THE TOUCHING

KAREN SARGSYAN
THE TOUCHING

KAREN SARGSYAN
WINNER THIEME ART AWARD
2007, ART AMSTERDAM

THIEME ART, DEVENTER

The Utopia of a Cut-Out King: Karen Sargsyan

Since being accepted at the Rijksakademie in Amsterdam, Karen Sargsyan, has had a whirlwind career. His baroque, fragile, yet technically highly refined paper sculpture groups appeal to the imagination. They are «tableaux vivants» in which viewers discover the theatres of comedy and tragedy, as well as countless hidden histories.

By Ingrid Commandeur

We agreed to meet in a specific space at the Rijksakademie, which Karen Sargsyan, who was born in 1973 in Jerevan, Armenia, is temporarily using to build a large new installation for the academy's «Open Ateliers 2007». In the space is a large, round white platform, on which six life-size paper dolls seem to be dancing at the gates of Hades, in strange rite of passage whose origins we do not recognize. These beings all have the same mask-like countenance – so characteristic of Sargsyan's work. Scattered on the floor are more objects, which look like brushes or candles, masks, or just common utensils. In the middle of the scene, on a pedestal, one figure towers high above all the others. He has been hit square in the chest by several arrows. It is a dramatic spectacle, for although the arrows are of paper, they still seem to have bored right into the 'flesh' of their target. And there are other less than cheerful aspects of what at first seems like a clownish carnival procession. Between the figures, as they circle around a central axis, lies a brown, wolf-like animal, chewing on a head. What makes the real impression is how human the paper figures seem to us. They have been constructed, like straw dolls, from several layers of paper. All the characters stand frozen in their poses, but we can only imagine it as a fleeting moment. Snap your fingers and they will come to life, step down from their platform and march in procession through the Rijksakademie.

'I will turn it on', says Karen Sargsyan, and the little group comes to life. The platform turns like a carousel, with the sound of Chinese children's songs in the background. The paper figures are built on 'skeletons' of steel wire, letting them gently surge and bob around a central point, flapping their arms and legs. They are now literally in motion, but because of their highly suggestive, dancing poses, it seems an addition that is hardly even necessary. The clothes they flaunt, hanging in layers around their bodies, are frayed, chewed up, eaten away. They might be costumes from long-gone ages, with puffy balloon trousers and sleeves, high rolled collars, head ornaments, frilled skirts, capes and loose, draped pieces of fabric. These, and such accessories as plumes on a hat or a brush in a hand, cause each figure to move quite differently. They parade around as if they had been completely aware of their audience right from the start. If their movements are sometimes contorted, they are always theatrical.

Beside the round platform is a rostrum, with a microphone, empty and silent. For whom does it wait? The rostrum reminds me of a speech given by the Italian cabaret performer, Beppe Grillo, in Rome, on the «Vaffanculo Day» (fuck-off day), which he organized. That day, Grillo managed to mobilize thousands of Italians. His web log attracts hundreds of thousands. 'Italian Politics held Hostage by a Comedian', read the newspaper headlines: by Grillo, the poseur, the troublemaker, the ultimate representative of the anti-establishment. The impotence of politics: is that what the out-of-place rostrum implies?

Sargsyan does not like to talk about his work. His answers to my questions were short, softly spoken. He preferred to let me do the telling. 'What story do you see in it?' he asked me. I mentioned potential connections to the work, rephrased my questions, tried to learn something about his life in Armenia, but for the purposes of our conversation, it seemed that his life only began when he was accepted at the Rijksakademie. He sketched only a summary picture for me of what went before.

In Jerevan, where he was born, Karen Sargsyan spent a few weeks at an art school, but could not find his footing. 'I couldn't do anything with what they were teaching there. I didn't think it was interesting. It was no good.' He subsequently attended a school for sports, then worked teaching sports (he later mentioned that his knowledge of anatomy was very useful) and as a boxer. He came to the Netherlands in 1998 because of political tensions and poor living conditions in Armenia. Sargsyan spent his first years in a centre for asylum seekers, where he again took up drawing and painting. 'I was mostly doing things at the level of semi-professional art clubs, until somebody advised me to apply to the Rijksakademie.' Although Armenian folk art does have a tradition in the making of paper dolls, Sargsyan says that he is not referring to traditions or art from Armenia, although he realizes that, in terms of figuration and technical refinement, he must have picked up something from them.

Theatre Inside Theatre

'For one theatrical King Lear, the world is made up of a life-threatening stairway, with steep wooden steps leading from hell to heaven – or the other way around, from heaven down to hell. The kingdom of the other old king looks like a room just after a party; the empty champagne bottles are still lying around, coloured streamers and flags flutter from the ceiling and here and there are scattered globes of the Earth, casually lying about.'[1] I read this quote in a newspaper, after my conversation with Sargsyan. Kester Frederiks was describing two different productions of Shakespeare's «King Lear». But all I could picture in my mind were the sculptures of Sargsyan, his heaven and hell, all those objects strewn around the floor, objects whose bright colours evoke a room where a carnival parade has just passed through. I see his characters as actors in a theatre, in their fairy-tale transcendence to heaven, or their terrible descent into perdition.

The reference to theatre is no coincidence. «Human Behavior», with which Sargsyan won the 2007 Thieme Award is comprised of a group of two figures standing on a round platform, with a kind of viewing box on wheels in front of it. Inside the box is a tiny theatre, with three smaller, 'dancing' characters made of paper. The whole thing is accompanied by music by Mozart. The installation, «History of a Sect, Don't Go Inside, Don't Touch» (2006) was literally constructed as a stage set, as a theatre.

Sargsyan's studio at the Rijksakademie is filled to the brim with paper dolls, large and small. The walls are hung with paper objects. Objects are littered about, apparently randomly, all over the floor. It is a complete paper universe, yet one we are not permitted to enter. Paper poles bearing paper cords bar the entrance, and it is from there that we can watch the performance. Looking closely, we see that this work also includes another material, in addition to paper. It is clay. There are several small artefacts made of clay dispersed around the floor, some of them unrecognizable bric-a-brac, some in the form of a door handle, handcuffs, a hook and so on. They are what remains of the work with which Sargsyan was accepted to the Rijksakademie. He had created small, technically refined sculptures by pressing all kinds of objects and technical paraphernalia into clay, leaving it unfired and building up from the impressions 'still lifes', in which objects and beings have fused and melted together.

Sargsyan saw and still sees this as a symbolic interpretation of the multilayered complexity of the influence that society exerts on individuals. Each person is a product of his or her social and cultural environment, the philosophy that underlies it, its norms, habits and conventions. This process of forming and being formed found a literal translation in these works in clay.[2] At the Rijksakademie, Sargsyan began searching for a way to express this process as if it were theatre, a grand opera of life. To this end, he experimented with photography, which in 2006 he combined with clay and paper in «Rehearsal». We see a photograph of a stage set, built to scale, peopled with paper masks and small figures, between which lie the clay artefacts. From there, the step was quickly made to his 'real life' installations with paper characters, including «History of a Sect, Don't Go Inside, Don't Touch». To quote his web log, 'I look at the influences that affect people the same way that I look at a theatrical production. On the one hand, I want my work to reflect this play or game, but I also want to show the reduction and the purification. My work is not a static image. It shows an active process that expresses this 'cleaning up'. My installations are a play in which the protagonists try to wipe 'the factories' off the playing field, as if the protagonists were holy beings in a theatrical production. This is why the objects made of clay are already reduced, as it were, to archaeological artefacts.'[3]

What would humanity be like if we were capable of extricating ourselves from conditioning, from being bound by environment and society? If such a 'true' person were to emerge, how would he look back on previous generations?

Tiny Souls and Hidden Saints

There is a world of ideas underlying Sargsyan's work, one that is hard to get a grip on, yet very particular. It is a world of good and evil, represented by gods that are not real gods, but beings that represent the pure and the good, and that lead people in a process of purification. There are unmistakable hints of Nietzsche in this process. In his theory of «Untermensch und Übermensch», Nietzsche described how 19th-century mankind, thrown off course by decadence and nihilism, needed to undergo a kind of purification, and to that end had to divest himself of religion and moral ideals – which he described as masks of selfishness, power mongering and resentment. Nietzsche wanted to free people, to allow them the ability to independently create their own values. The transcendent, the godlike, can be found in mankind, and mankind is able to transcend itself. For Sargsyan, this existentialist search for the true and good core of humanity is fundamental, and god and man (the large and small figures) are two sides of the same coin.

To quote a description of his work for «KölnShow 2» at the Christian Nagel Gallery: 'Silence, timelessness and fragmented nostalgia characterize the three-dimensional paper installations of Karen Sargsyan. (...) The installations serve as an open podium for ideas that refer to collective memories. The theme of the work is unmistakably the discord between culture and nature. At the same time, the ideal of paradise is far away.'[4] Romanticism in art is characterized by a large measure of individualism, irrationalism and an emphasis on the power of expression, emotion and our relationship to nature. It was romanticism that led to a revival of craftsmanship and folk art. In this sense, both in terms of content and in terms of attention to craftsmanship and handwork, Sargsyan's work fits into today's longing for the romantic, for nostalgia.

But Sargsyan himself does not refer to Nietzsche or romanticism. He is the epitome of the autodidact, someone who follows his feelings in all he does. He is not inclined to mention the names of artists, writers or musicians (in addition to movement, he has added music to his most recent work) who have inspired him. The only fellow artist he mentioned to me was Folkert de Jong: 'It's nice that he exists and that I have gotten to know him. Our work is related, but it is also totally different. The way I work is more philosophical. I try to present a certain condition of the soul.'

Perhaps this is why his work transcends the sensitivity to fashion that is inherent to nostalgia and the romantic. His Armenian background means that for him it is self-evident that he should seek deeper values in the human condition, for which he reaches back to essential stereotypes and imagination, of the kind stored in our collective memory. As such, his work indirectly opens a broad palette of associations and references for the spectator. Sargsyan creates almost classical sculptural groups, but overturns the idea of the static monument by using exceedingly fragile materials, such as paper and unfired clay. They are materials that in turn instantly recall the oldest of ways with which human civilization was passed down: paper from the Bible and the clay that formed the earliest images of man.

There is a baroque exultation to Sargsyan's monumentality, but by mixing that with theatrical elements, there are more new associations, this time with the «tableau vivant». These 'living paintings' were especially popular among the 18th and 19th-century working classes for festival evenings and political gatherings. Unmoving, costumed people would stand in symbolic arrangements, with props providing a decor. The scenes were arranged behind closed curtains. When everyone was in the right position, the curtains would open and the audience could look, for a maximum of about two minutes. «Tableaux vivants» often expressed social issues and presented an ideal solution: this is reality, but «this» is how it should be. This is equally true in Sargsyan's case, albeit that he makes a conscious masquerade of reality. As he once poignantly phrased it on his web log, 'The idea behind my work is utopian, and in that sense, it is theatrical as well. This way of working winks an eye at the performance of my work and creates, as it were, a theatre within a theatre.'

Notes

1. Kester Frederiks, 'Lear als gedoemde. Lear als bittere nar', «NRC Handelsblad», 5 October, 2007.
2. Sargsyan calls them 'the factories', and they reappear in rudimentary form in all his later paper installations.
3. See Karen Sargsyan's web log: www.karensargsyan.web-log.nl
4. Press release for «KölnShow 2».

This text was published before in Metropolis M Tijdschrift voor hedendaagse kunst No. 6, 2007/ 2008.

THE TOUCHING
THEORY OF ART
HAMLET
WHERE WERE YOU
SUSHI AND THE KING
LET ME SWEEP THE DECORATIVE GODS,
AND DECORATIVE TRUTHS
LEAVE ME ALONE AND CUT YOURSELF
SHELTER
HUMAN BEHAVIOR
IN BETWEEN MOMENTS
OUR GODS
HISTORY OF A SECT, DON'T GO INSIDE,
DON'T TOUCH
INTRIGE
REHEARSAL
OPERA

THE TOUCHING

2007 / INSTALLATION / WOOD / IRON / PAPER /
SOUND AND STIRRING SYSTEM
390 X 400 X 400 CM

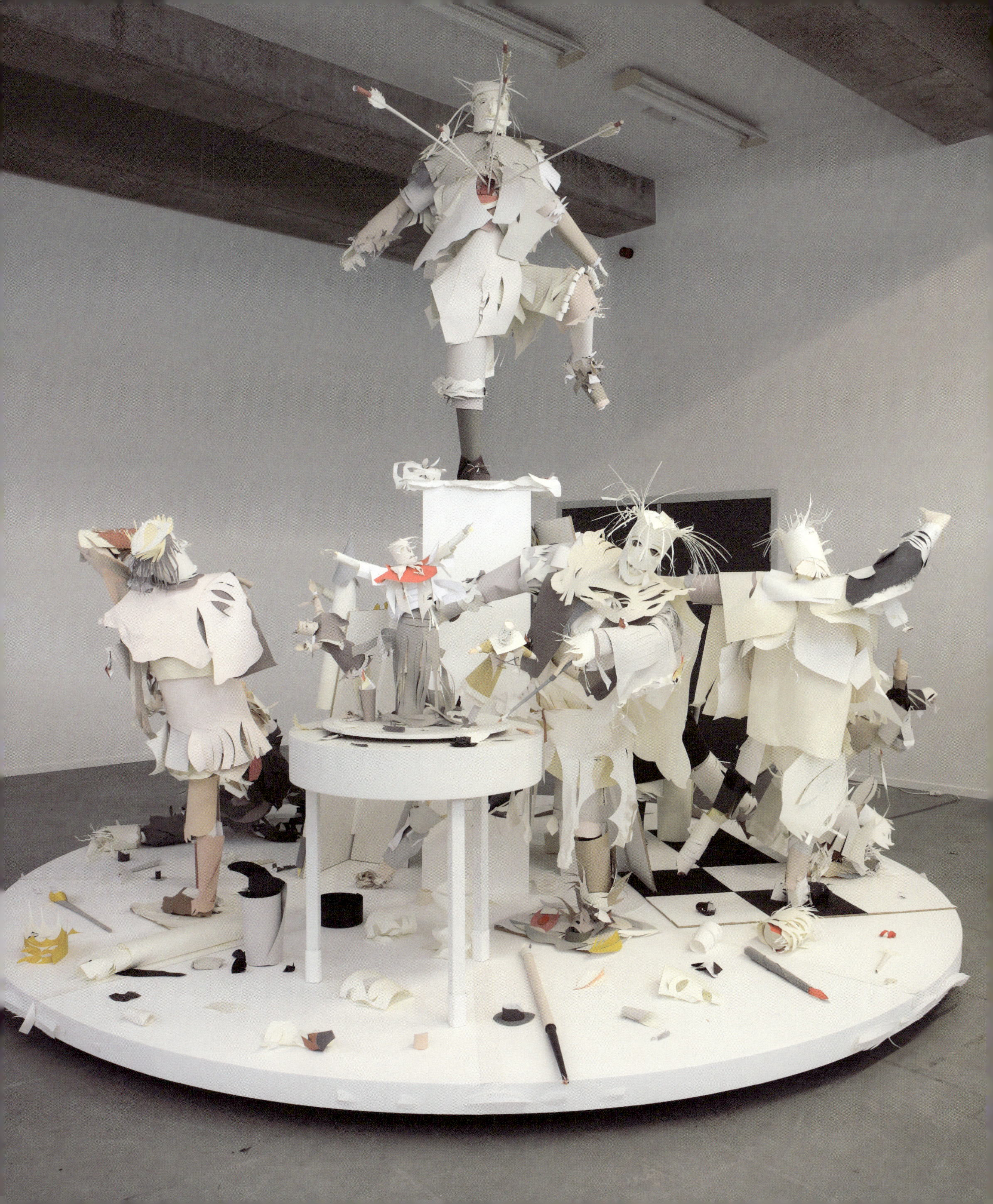

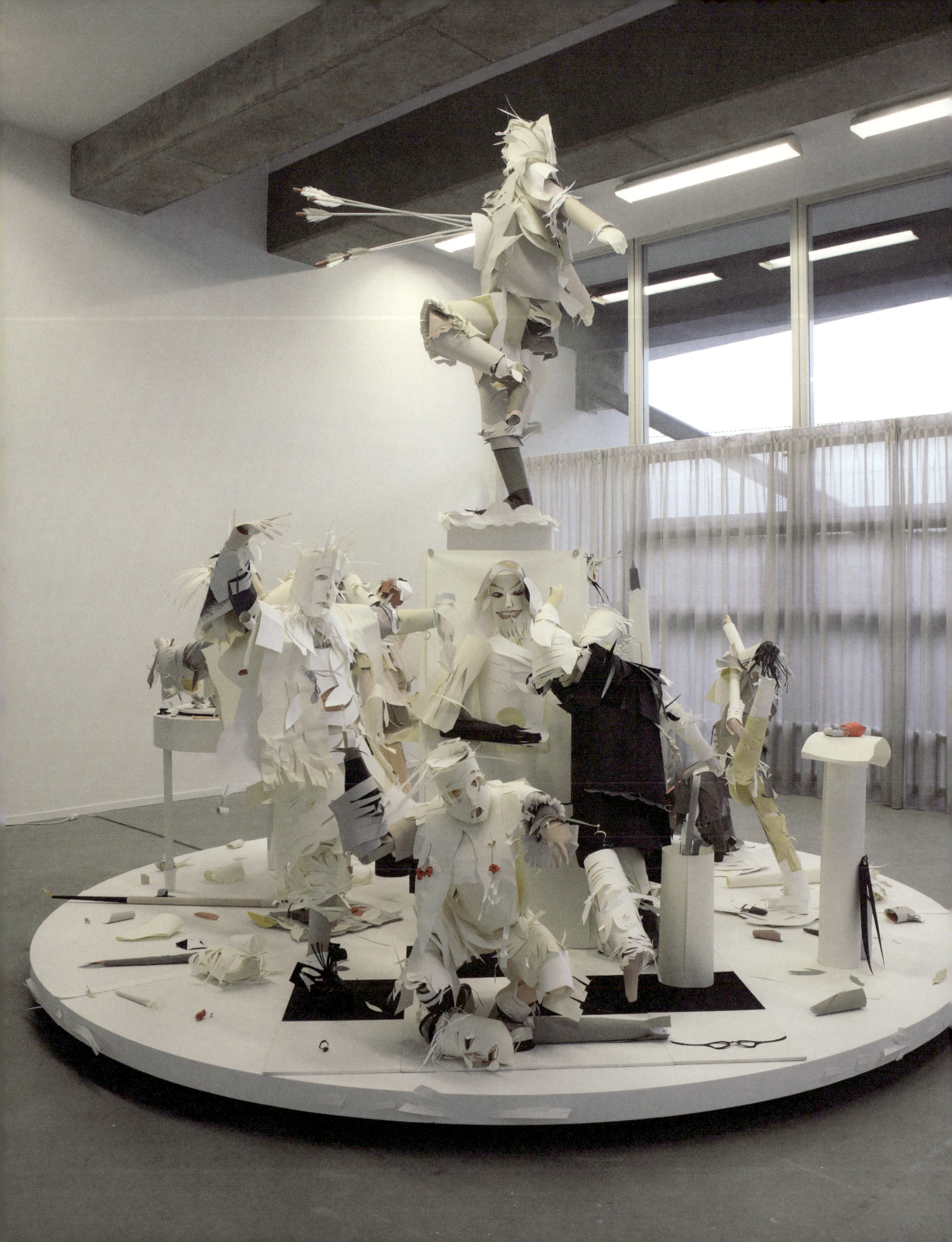

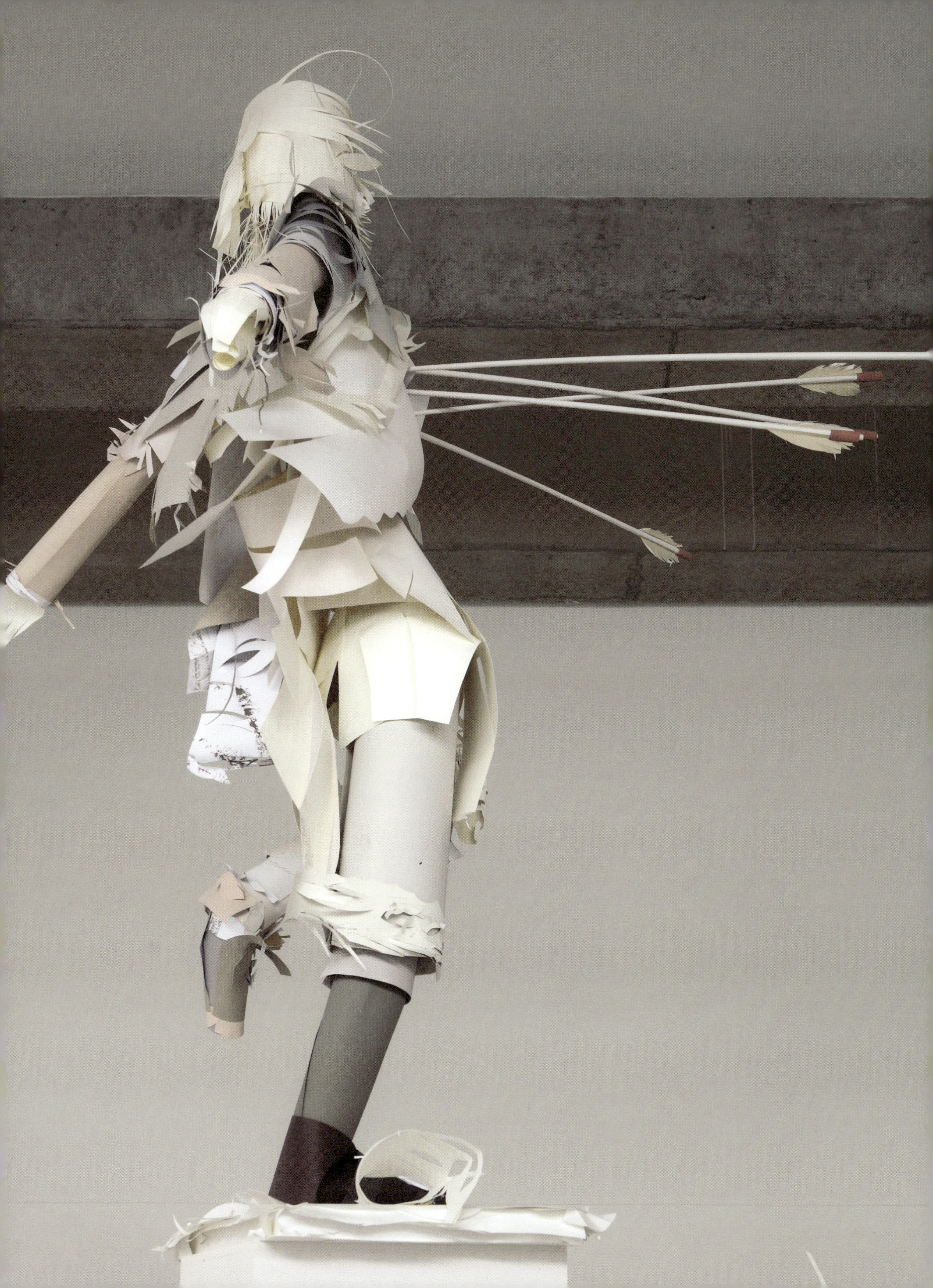

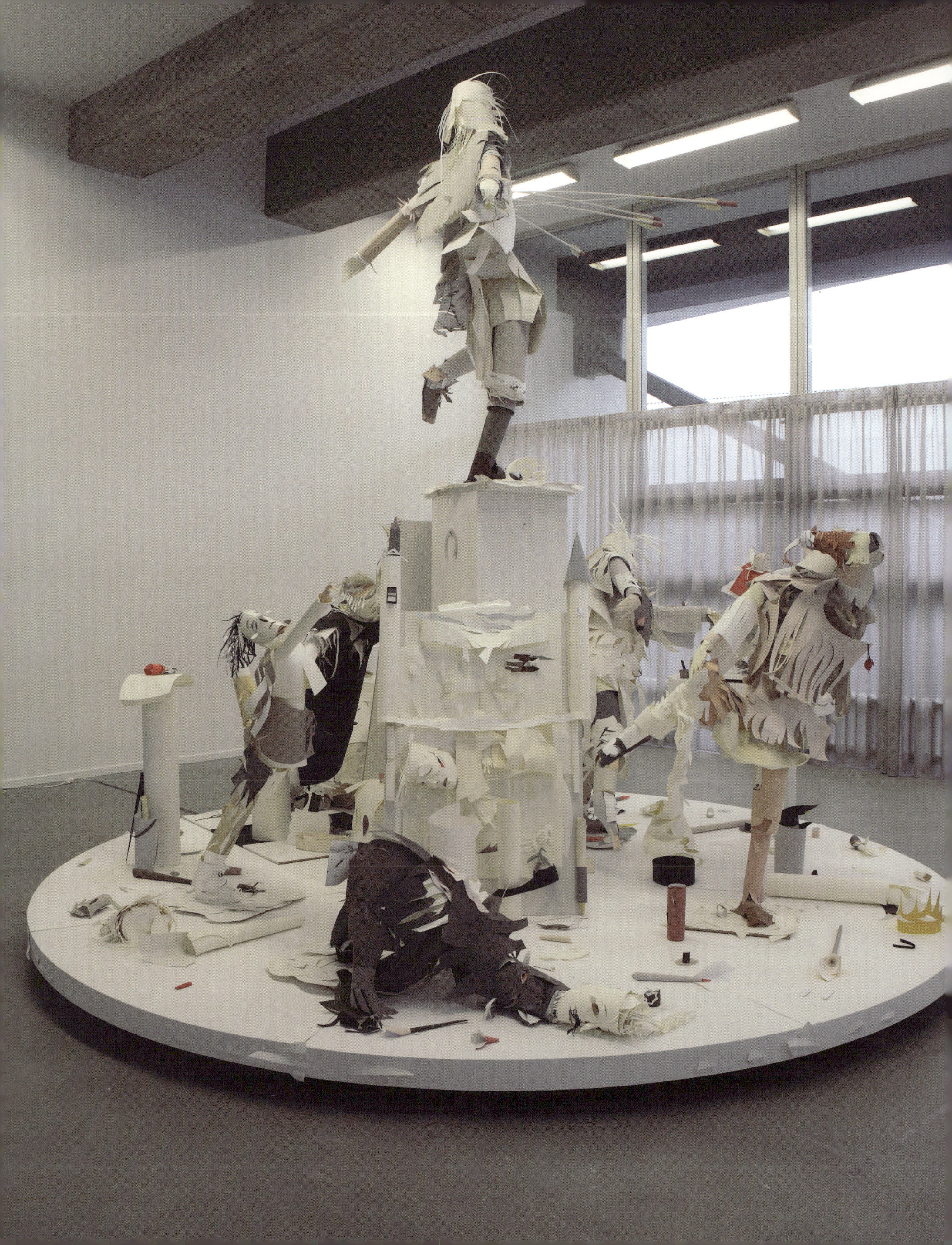

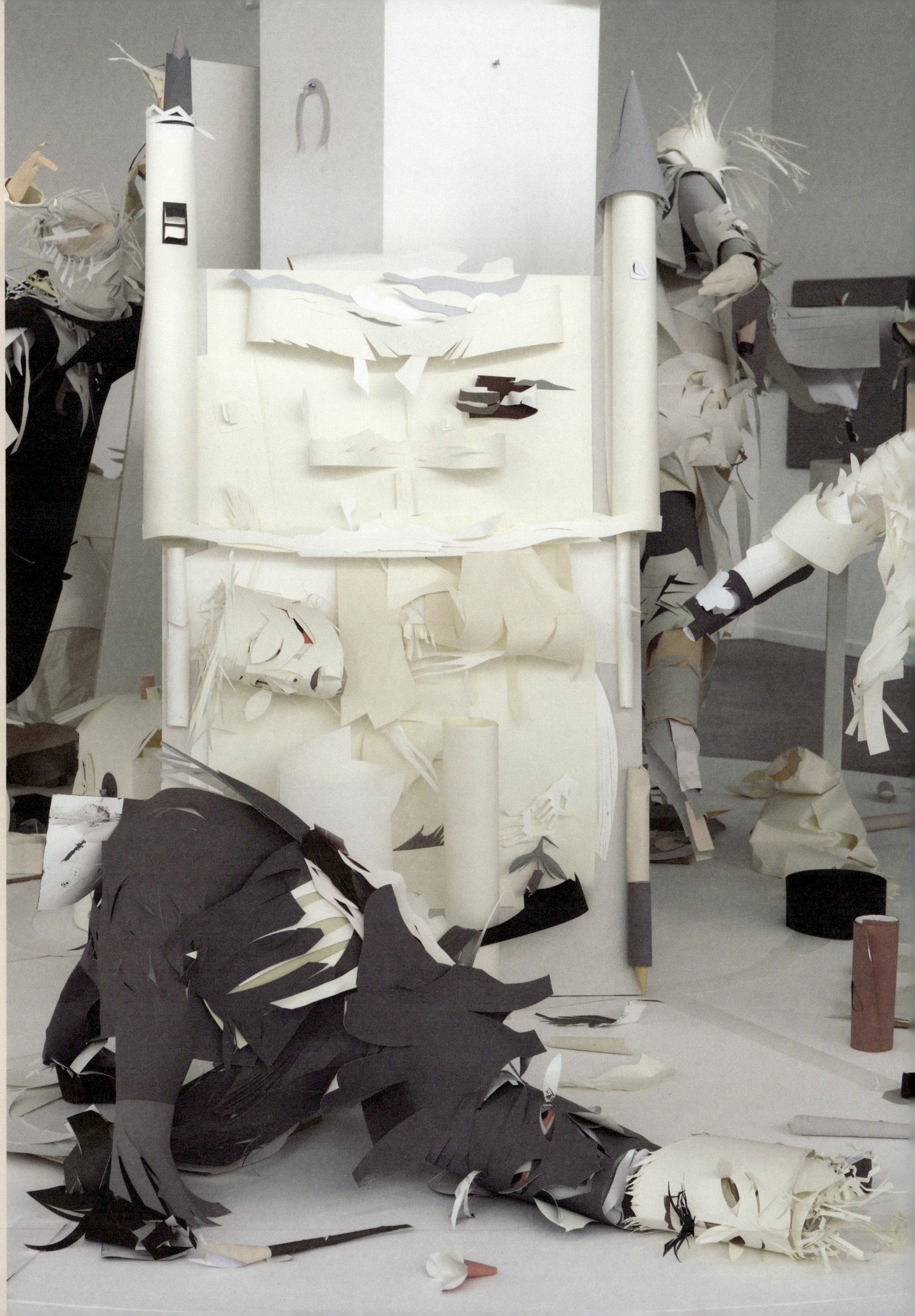

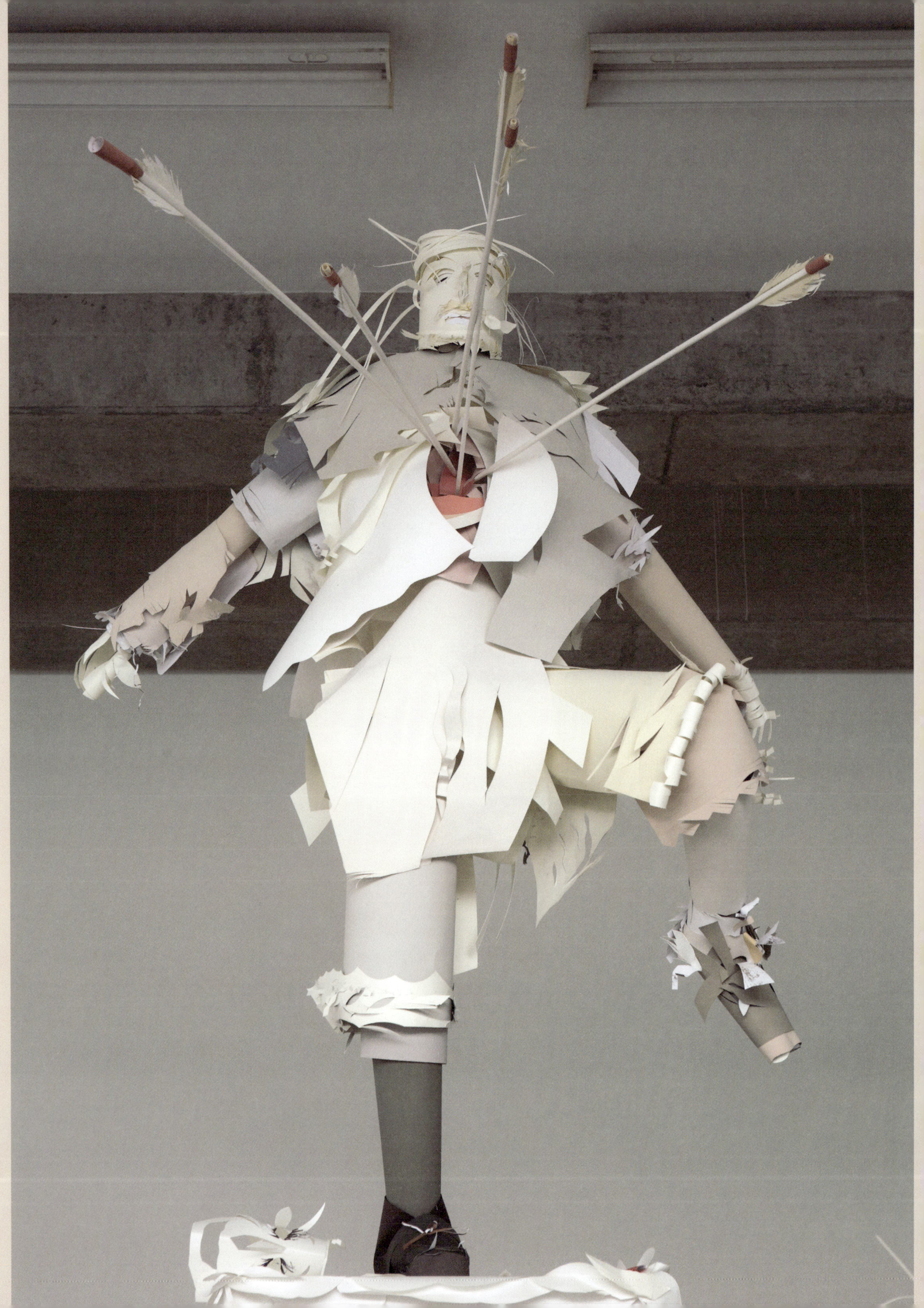

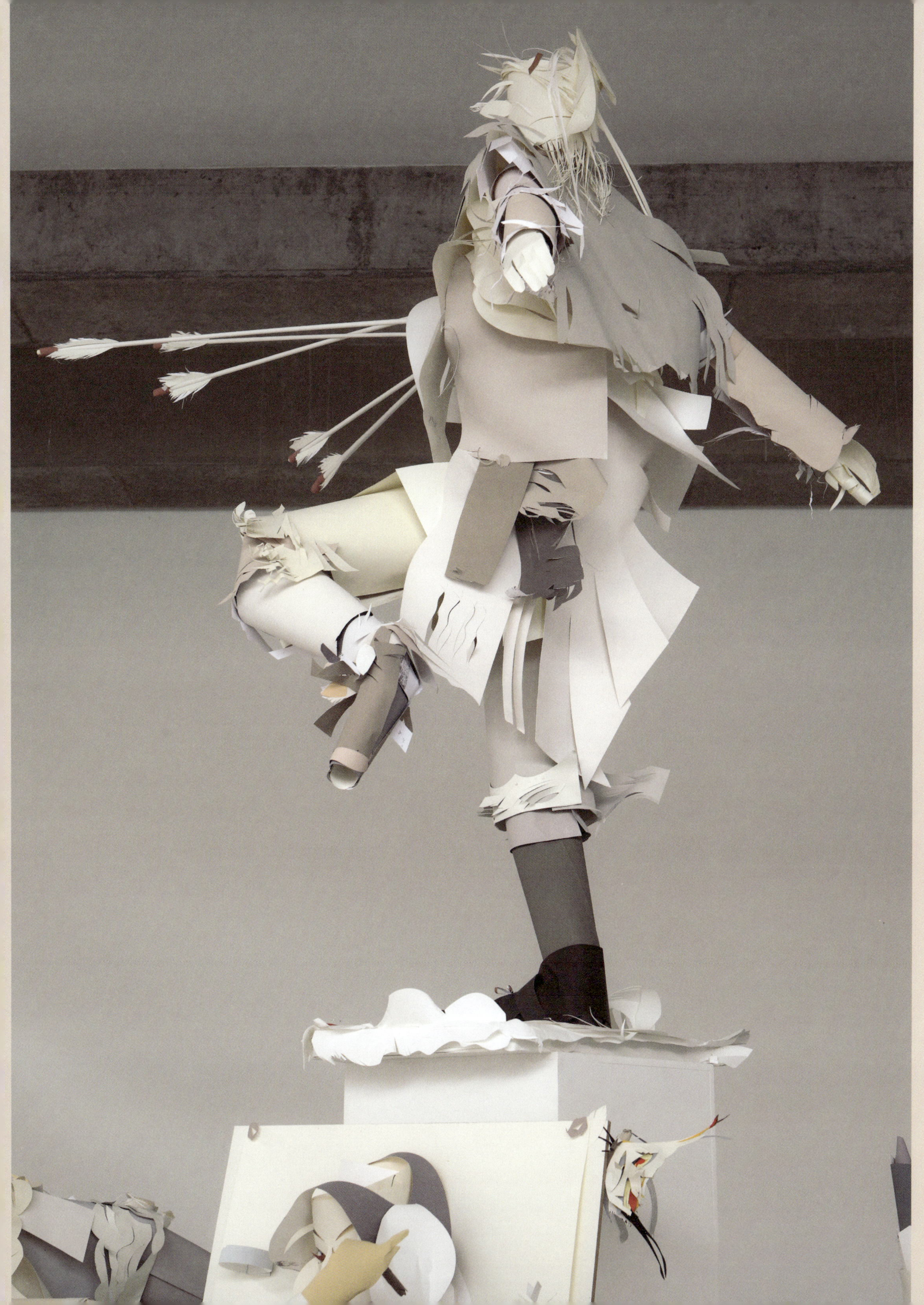

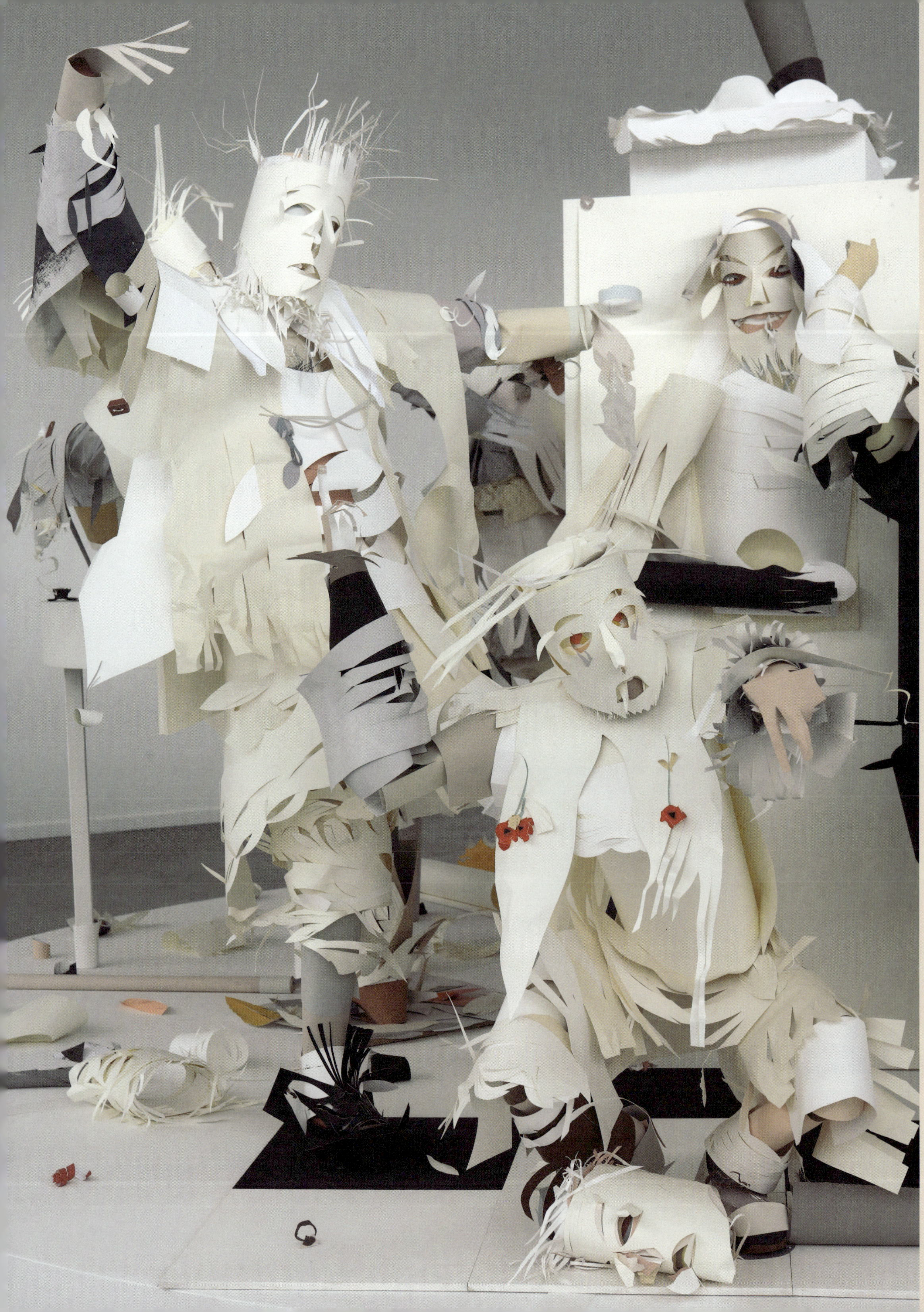

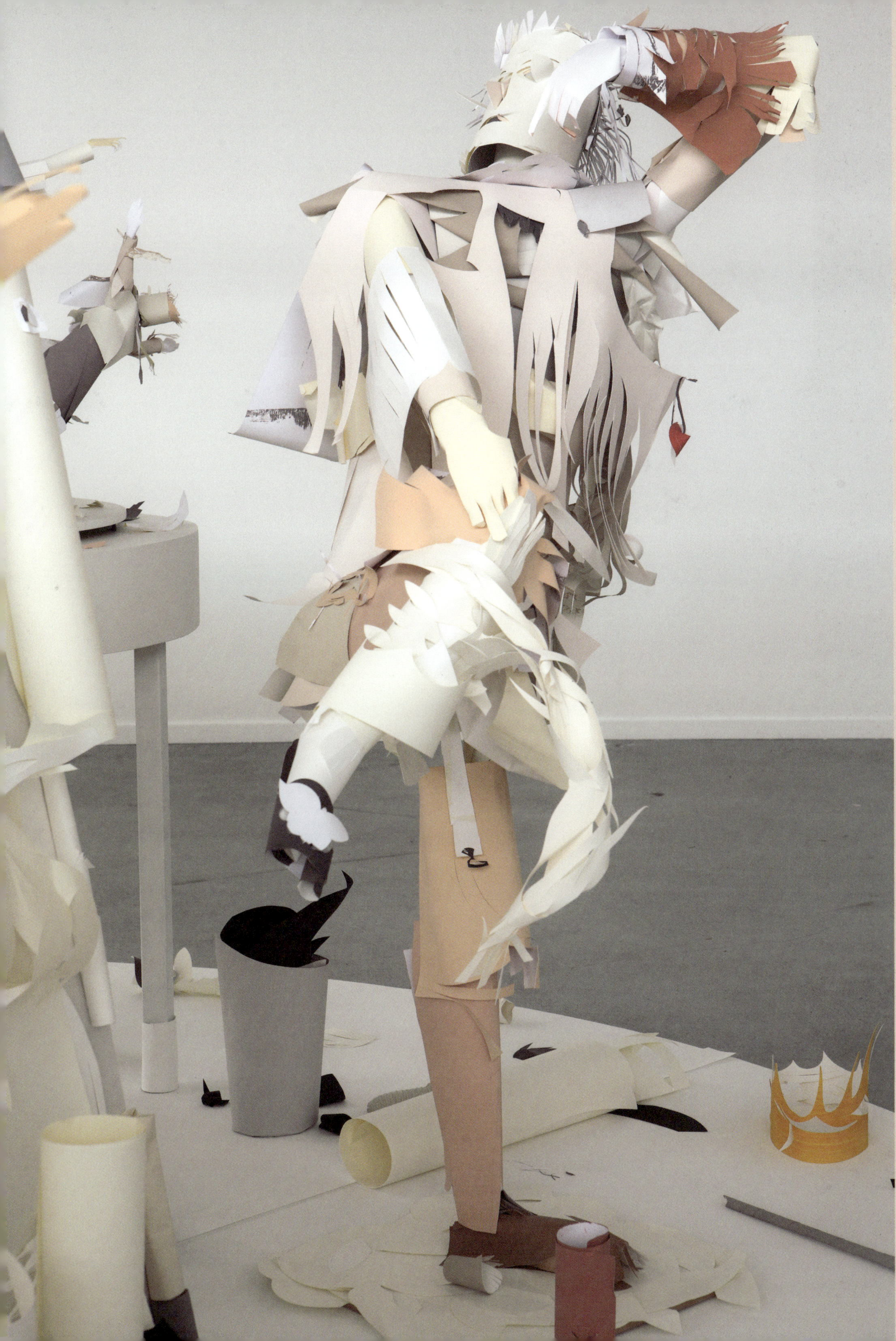

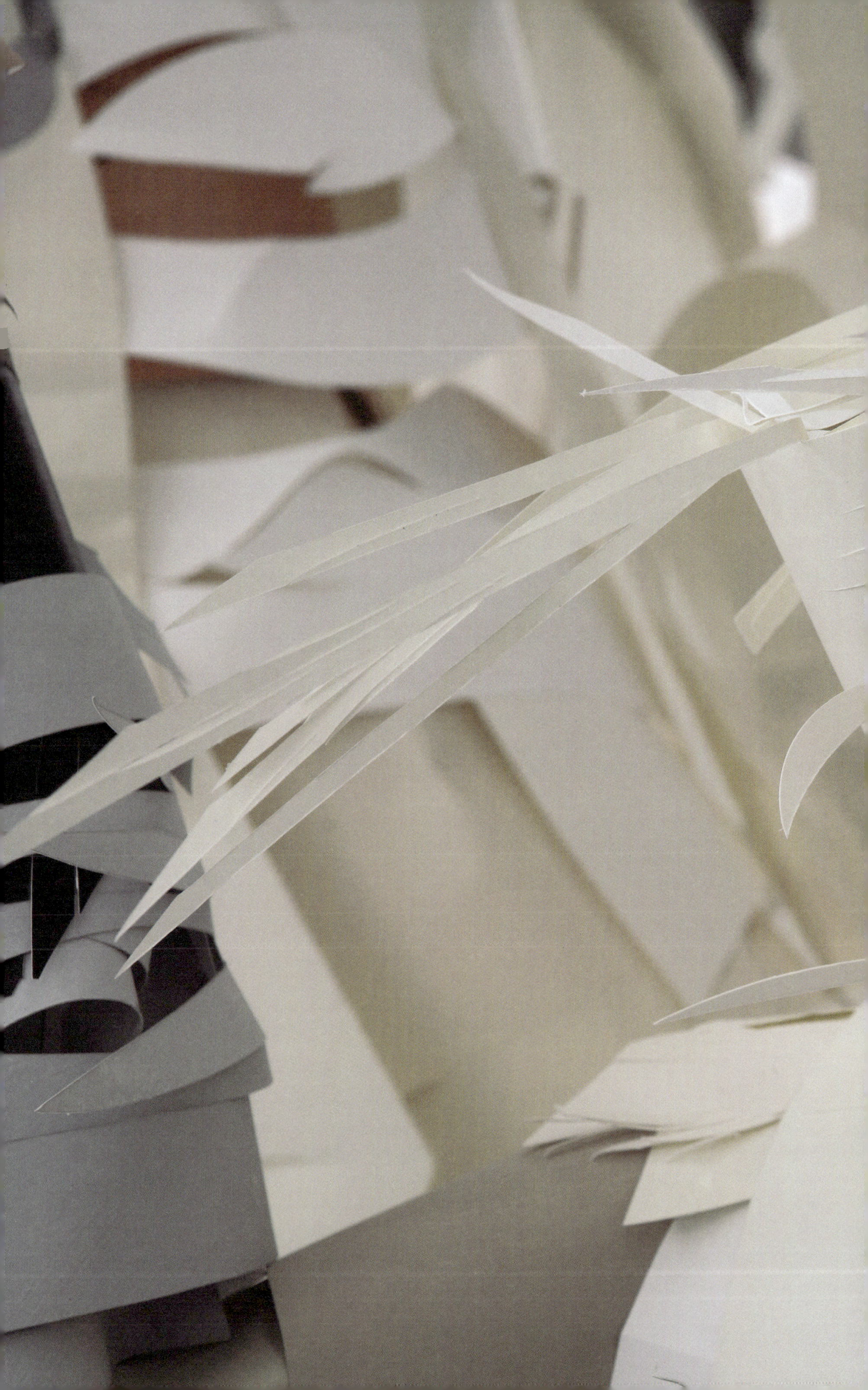

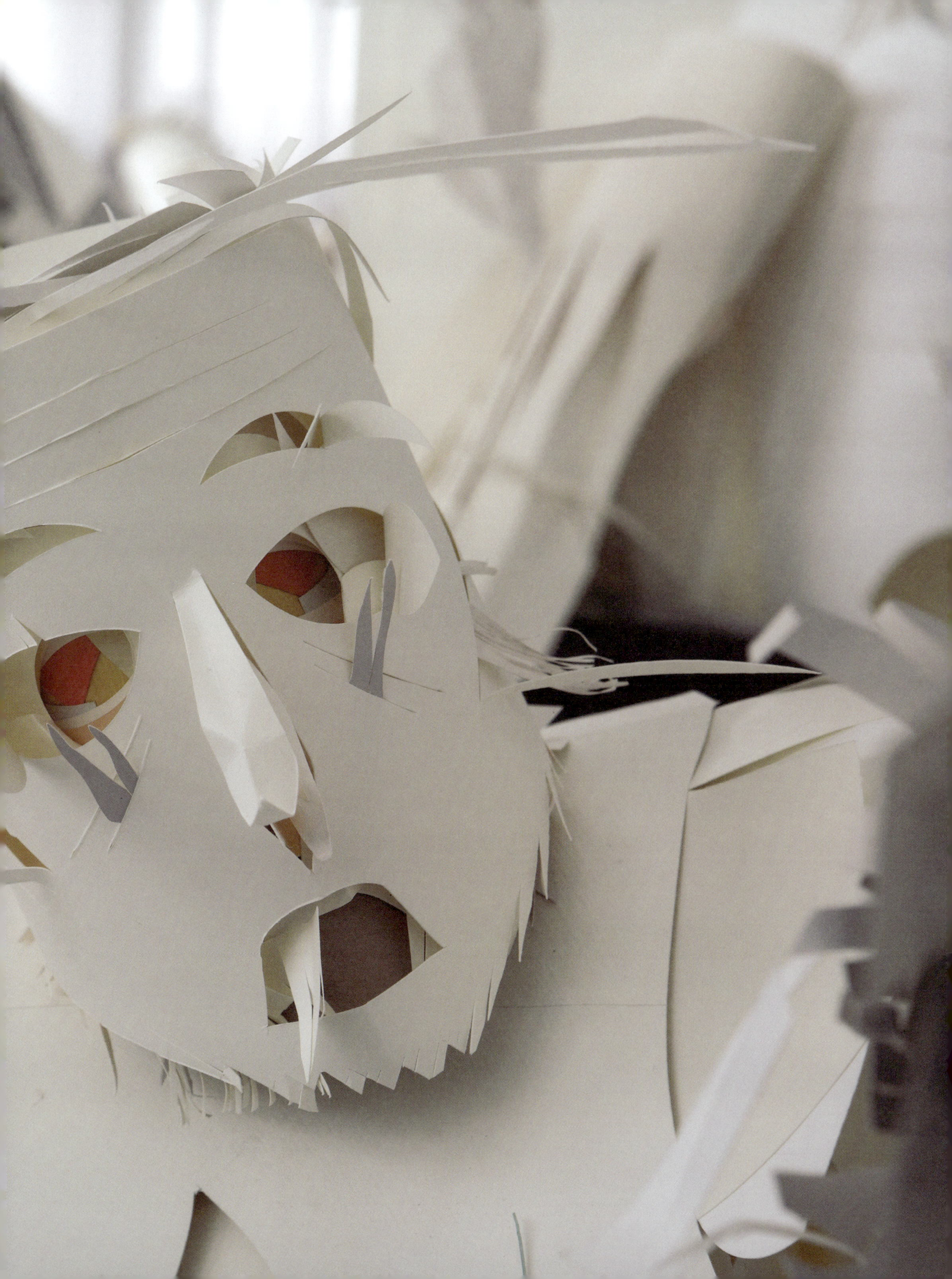

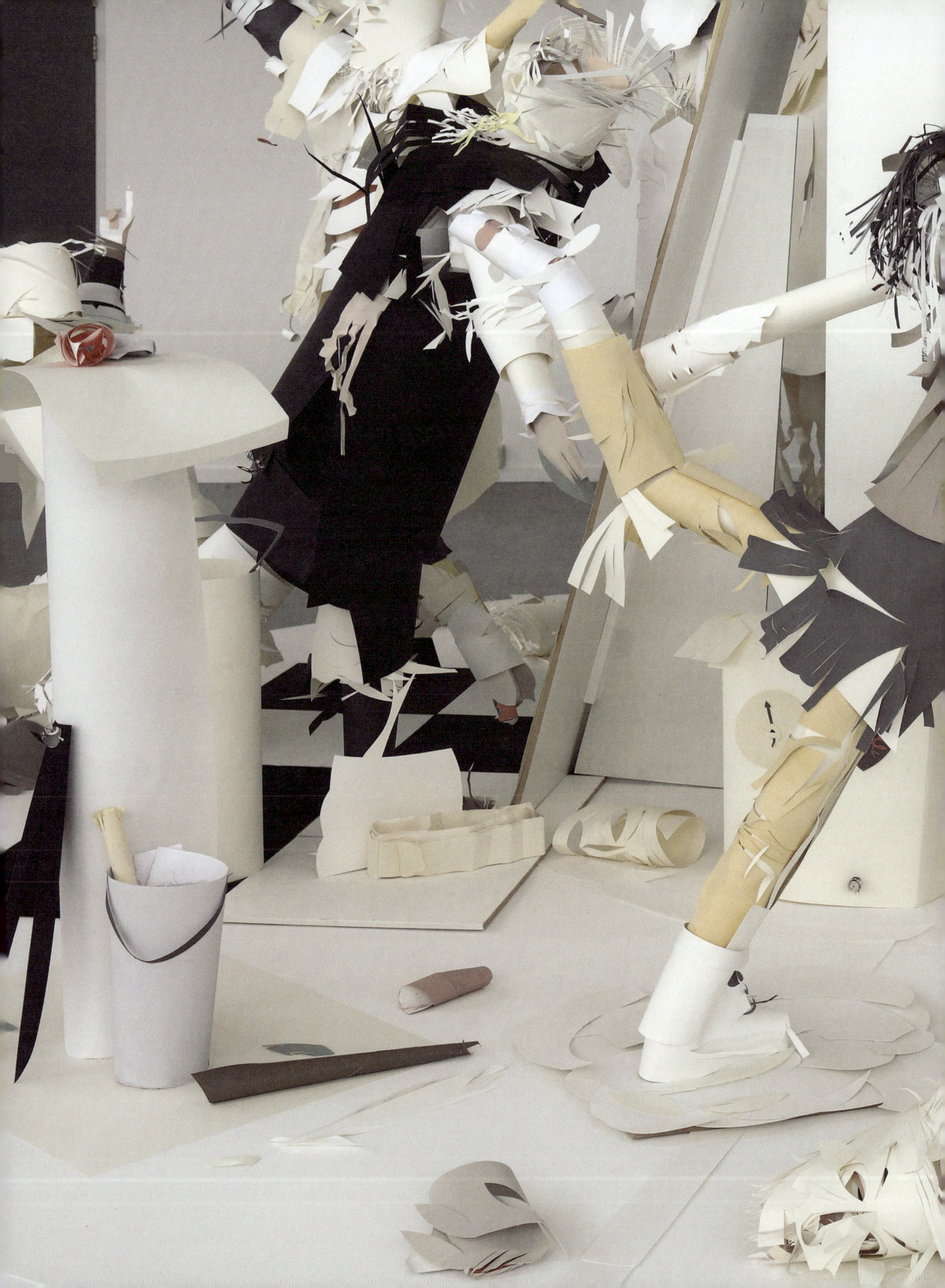

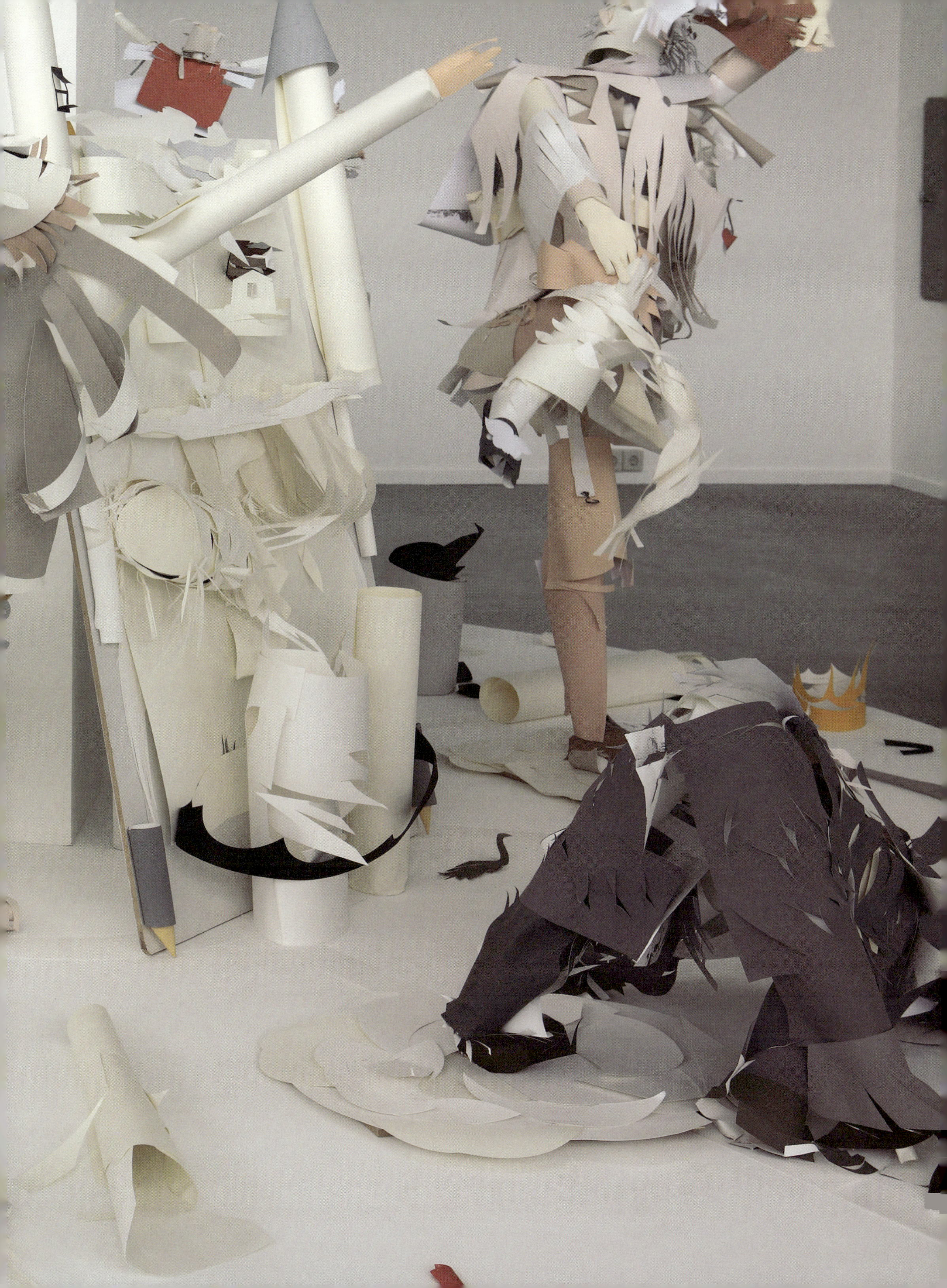

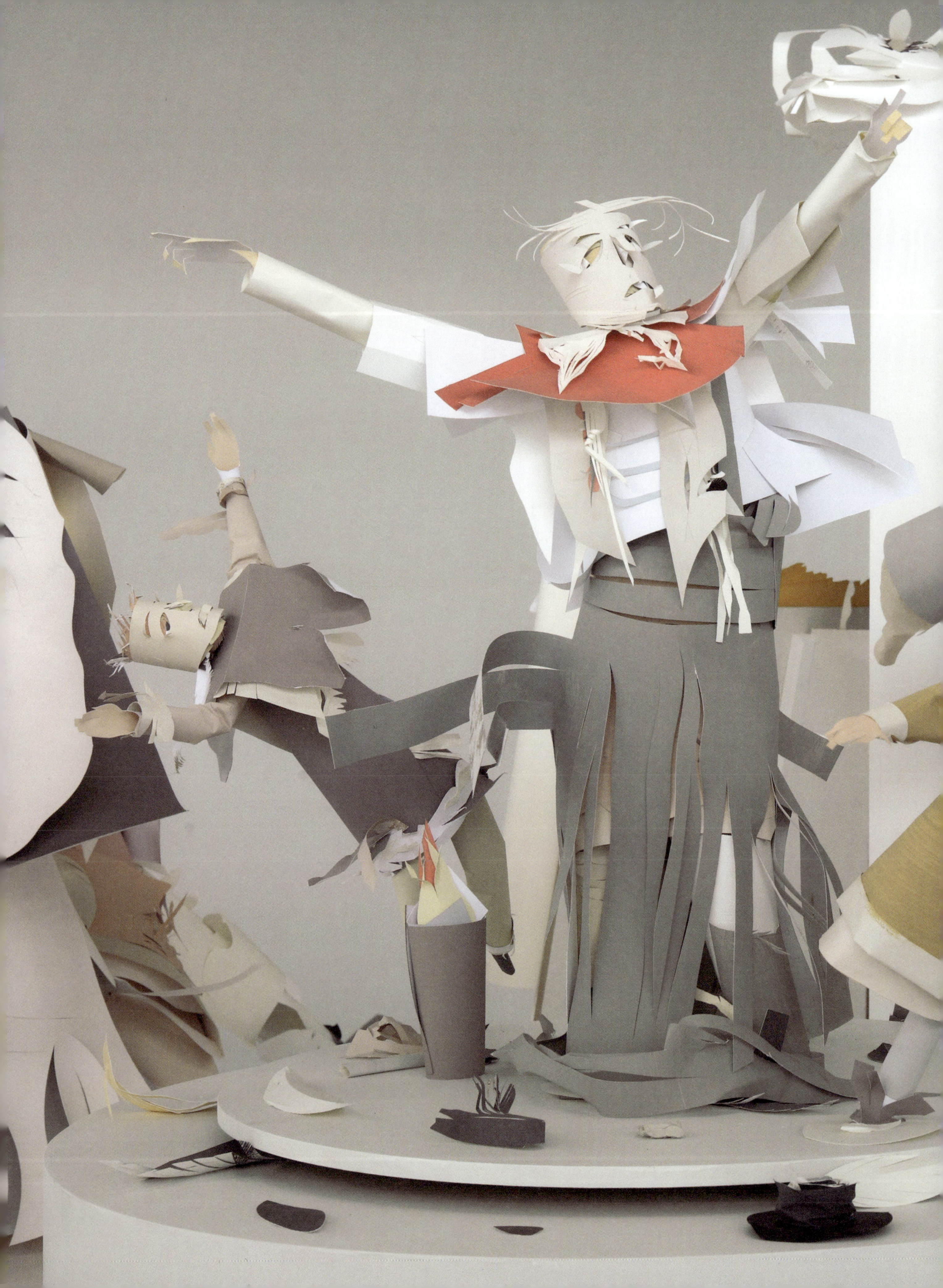

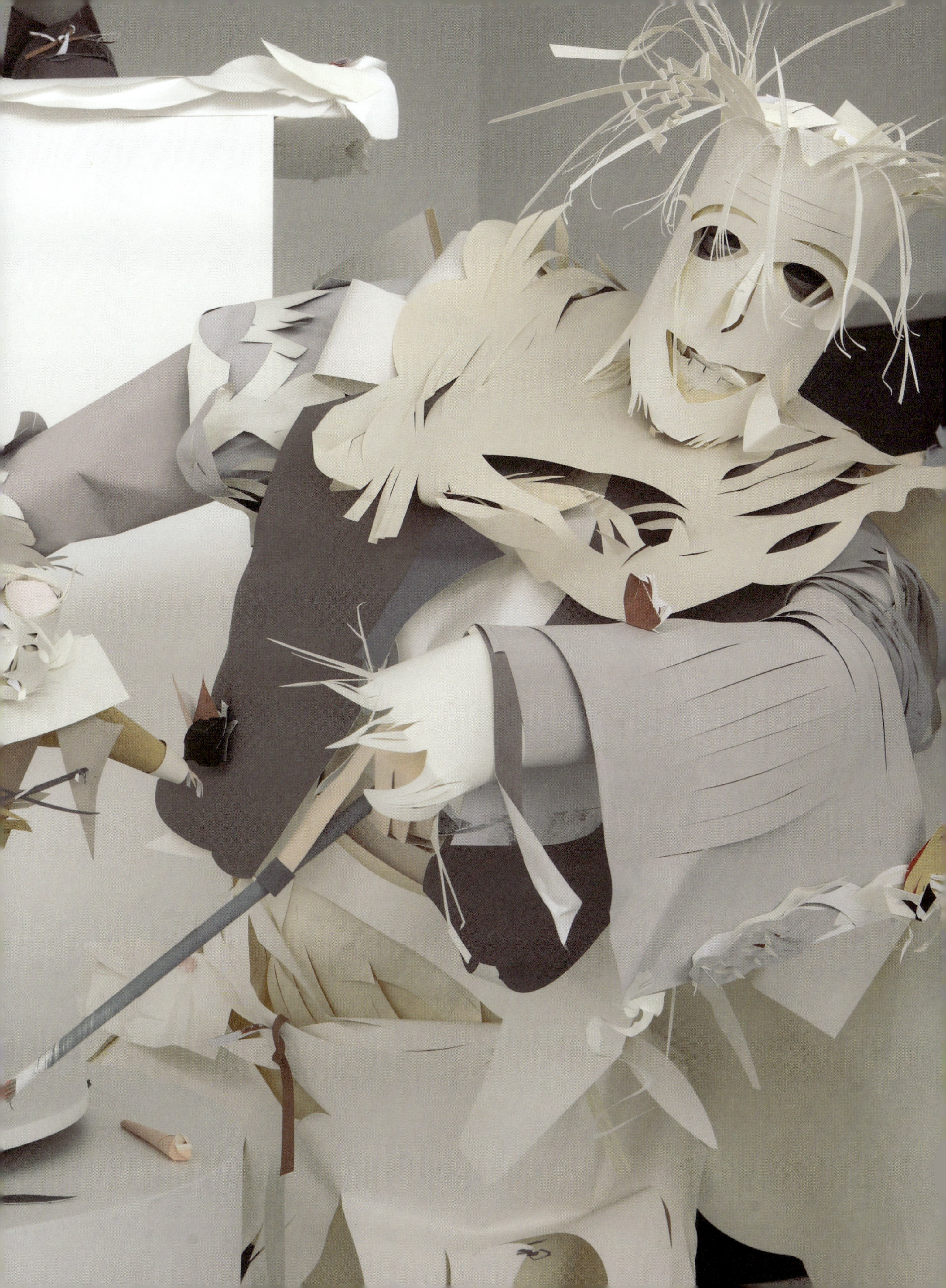

THEORY OF ART

2008 / INSTALLATION / WOOD / IRON / PAPER
200 X 420 X 230 CM

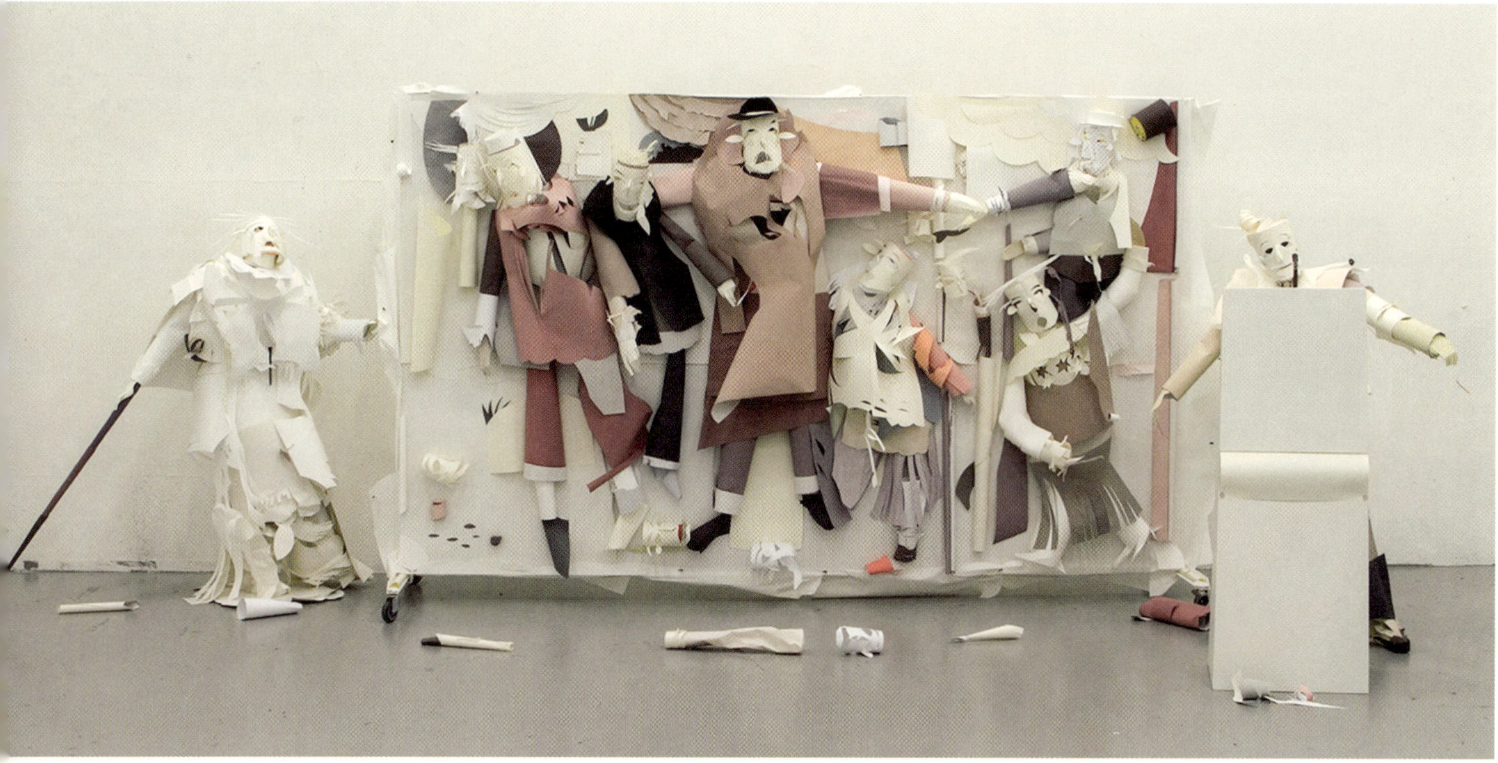

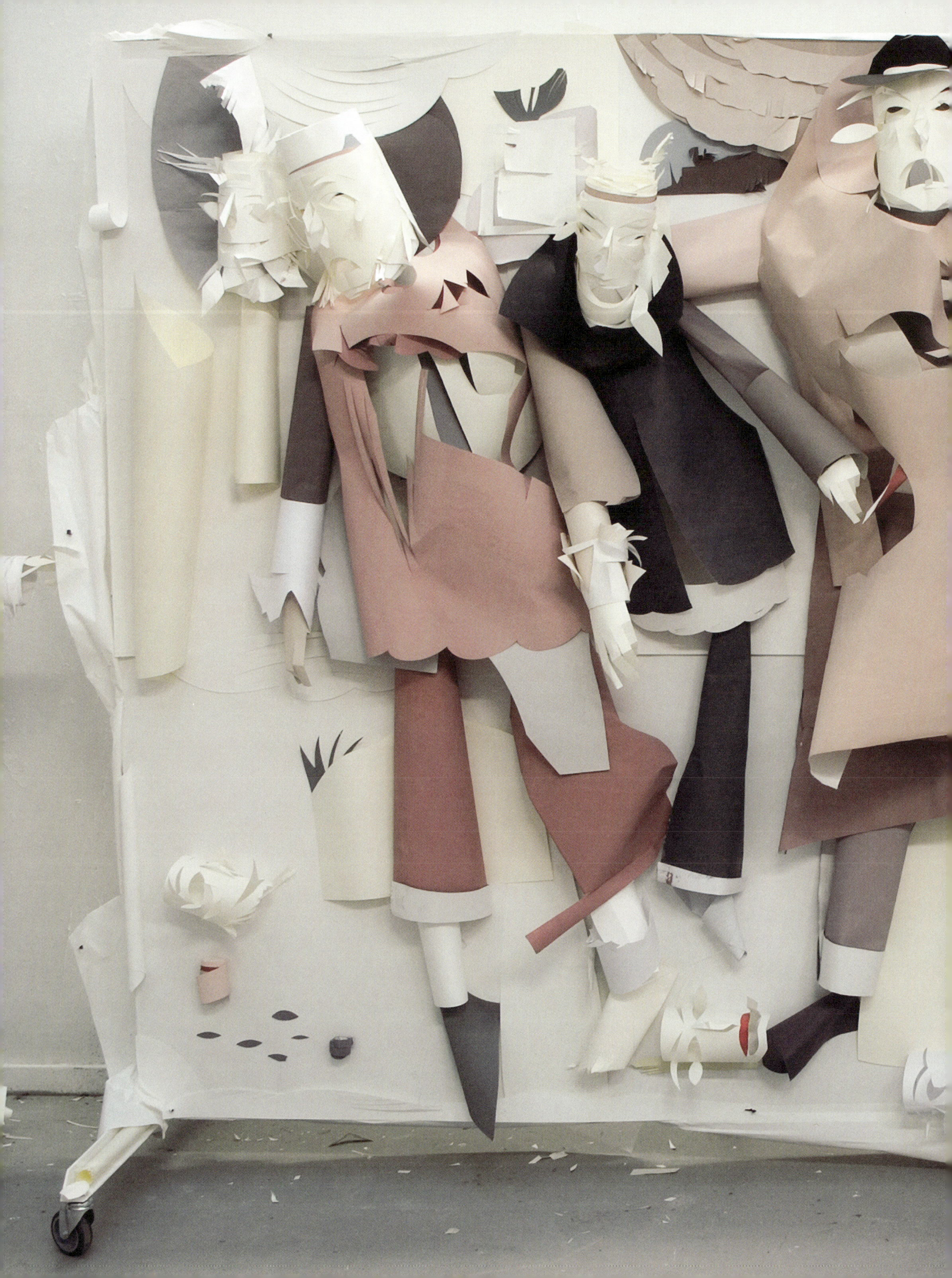

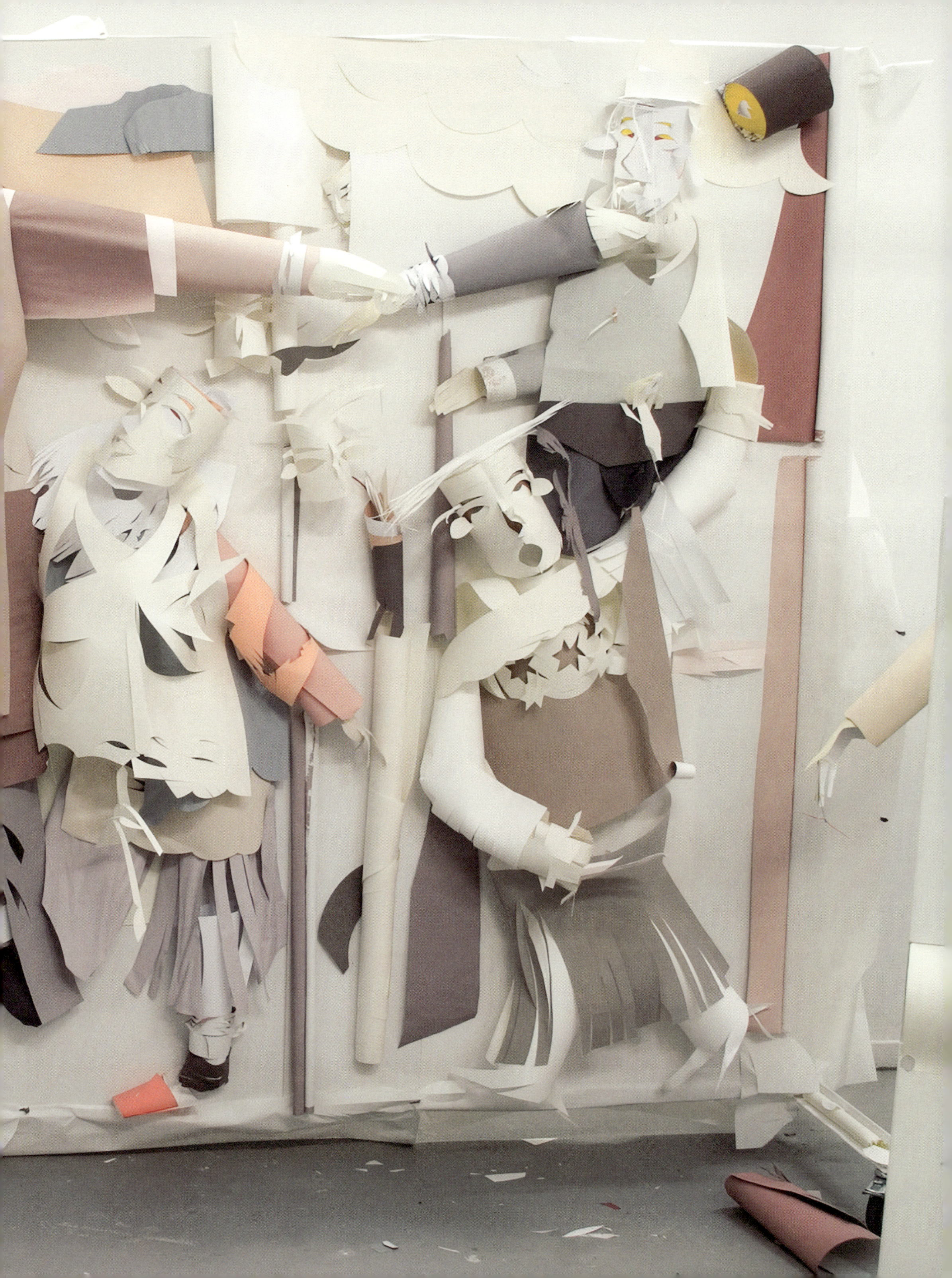

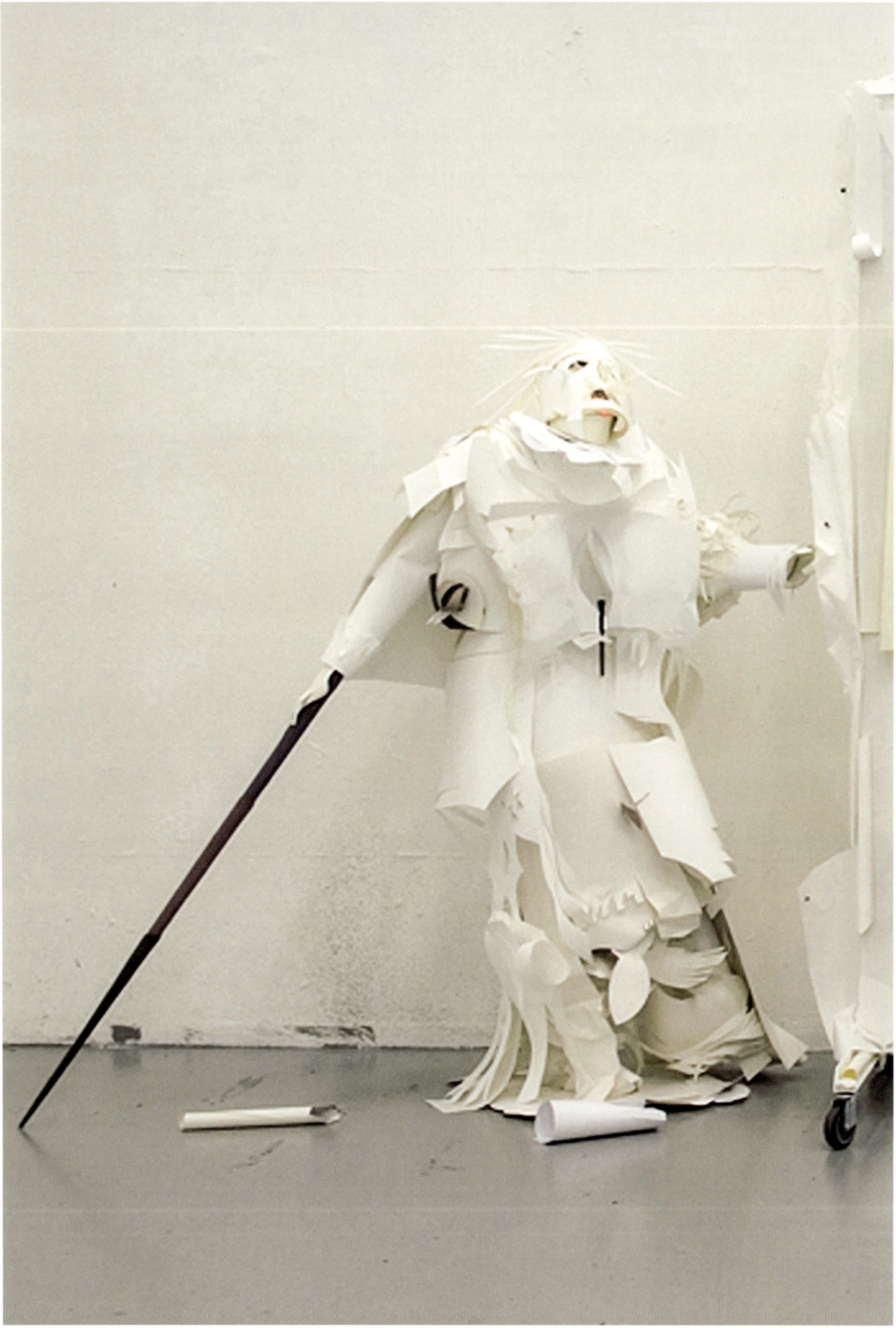

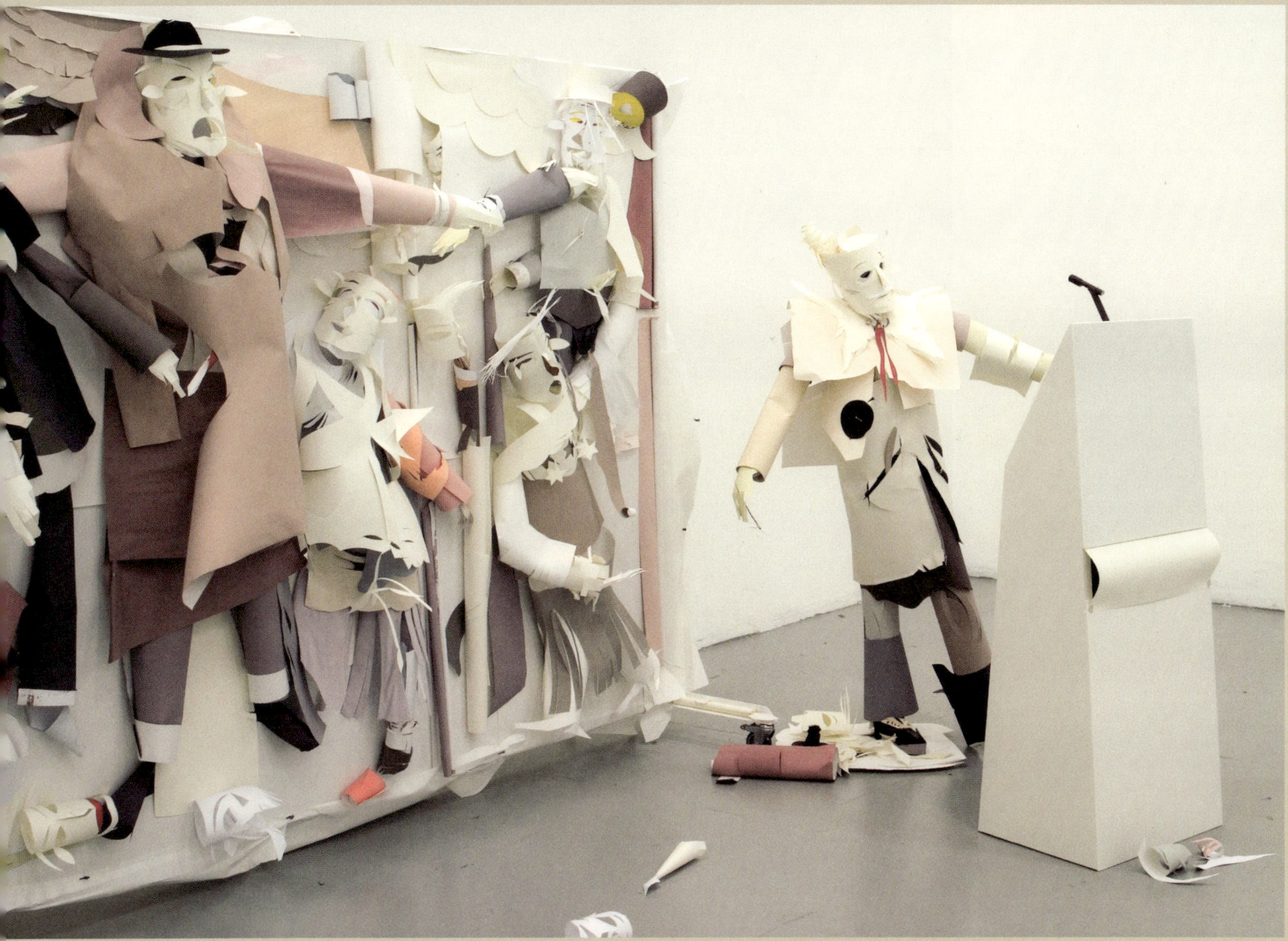

HAMLET

2008 / INSTALLATION / WOOD / IRON / PAPER
190 X 310 X 320 CM

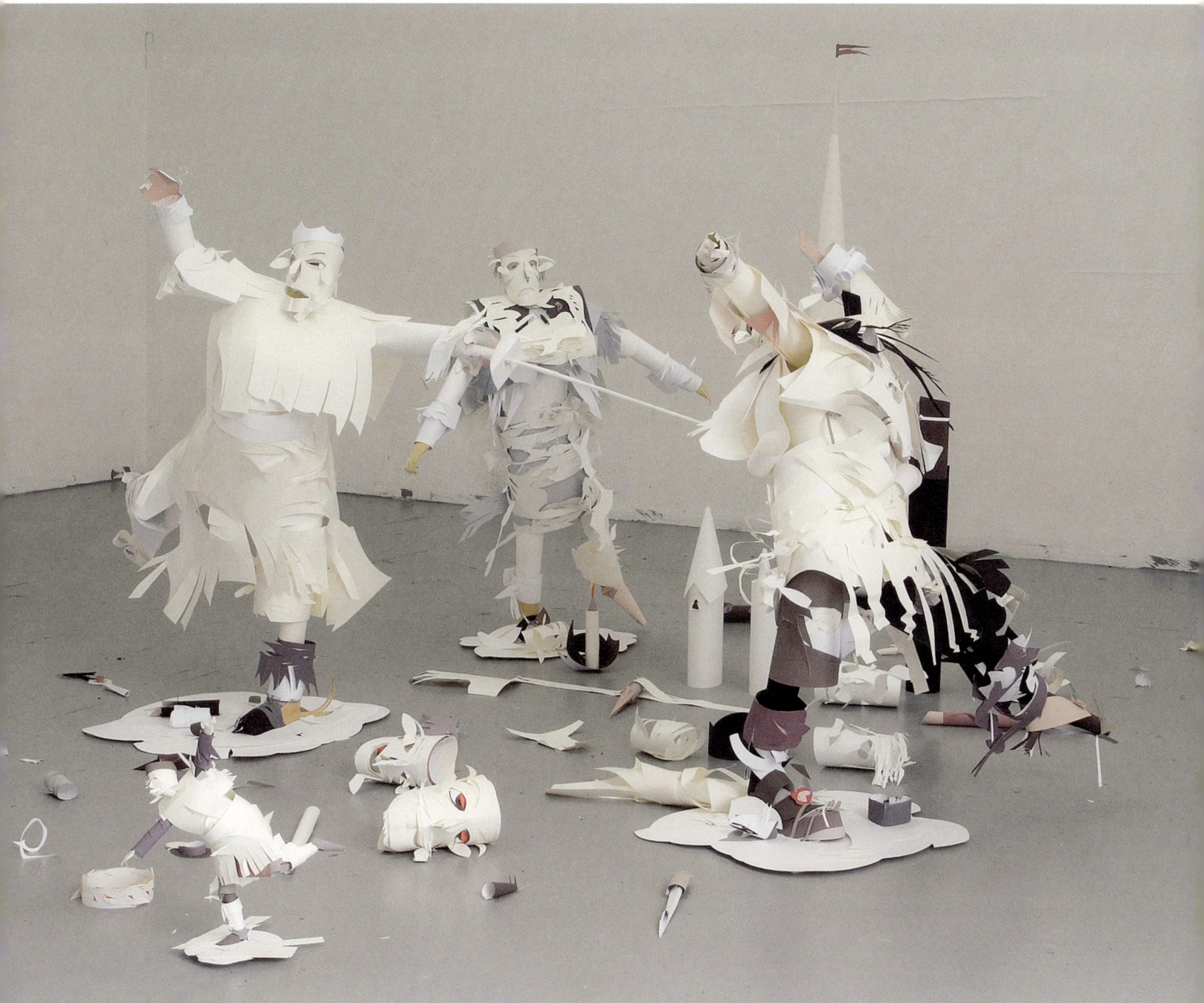

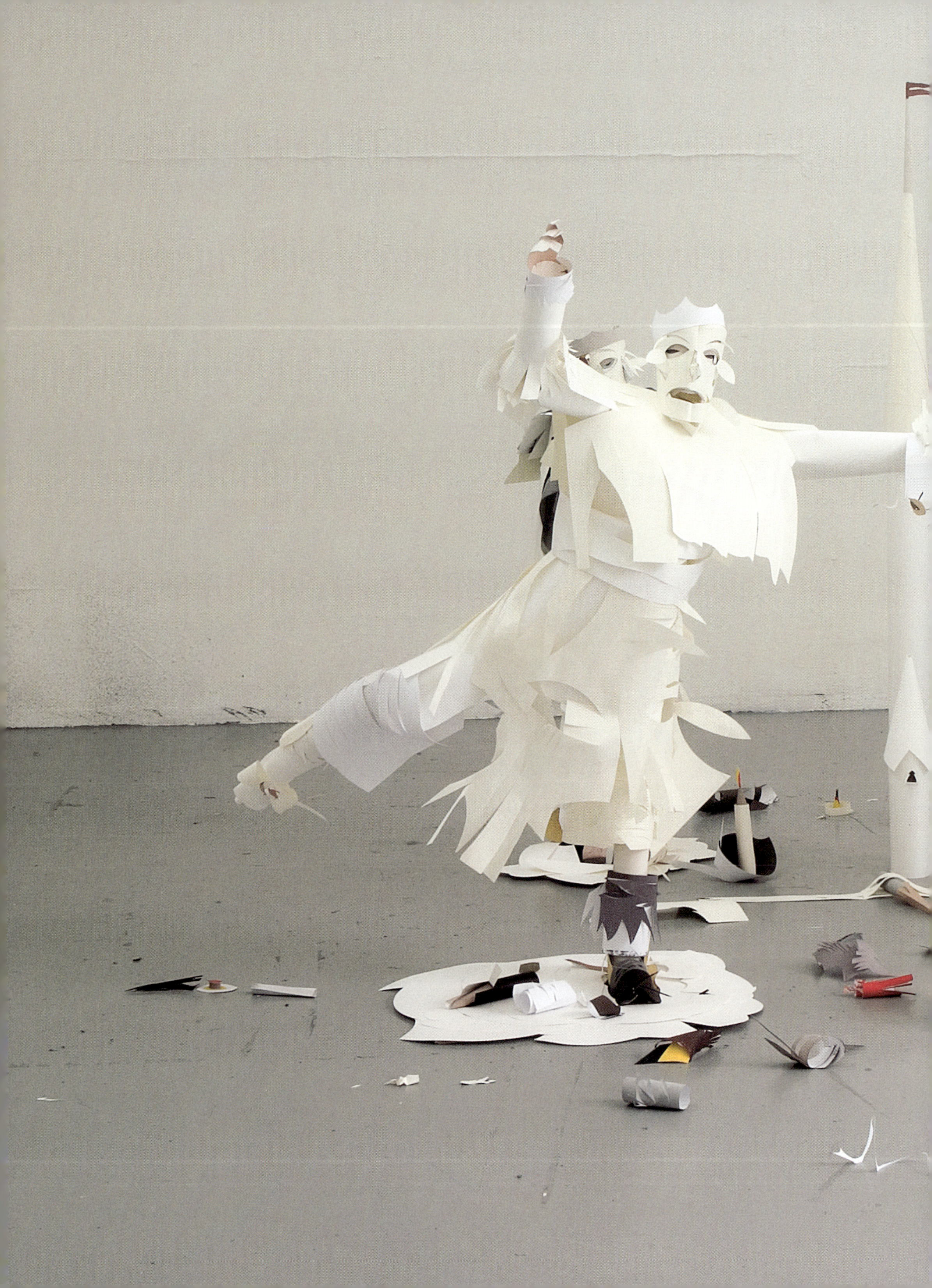

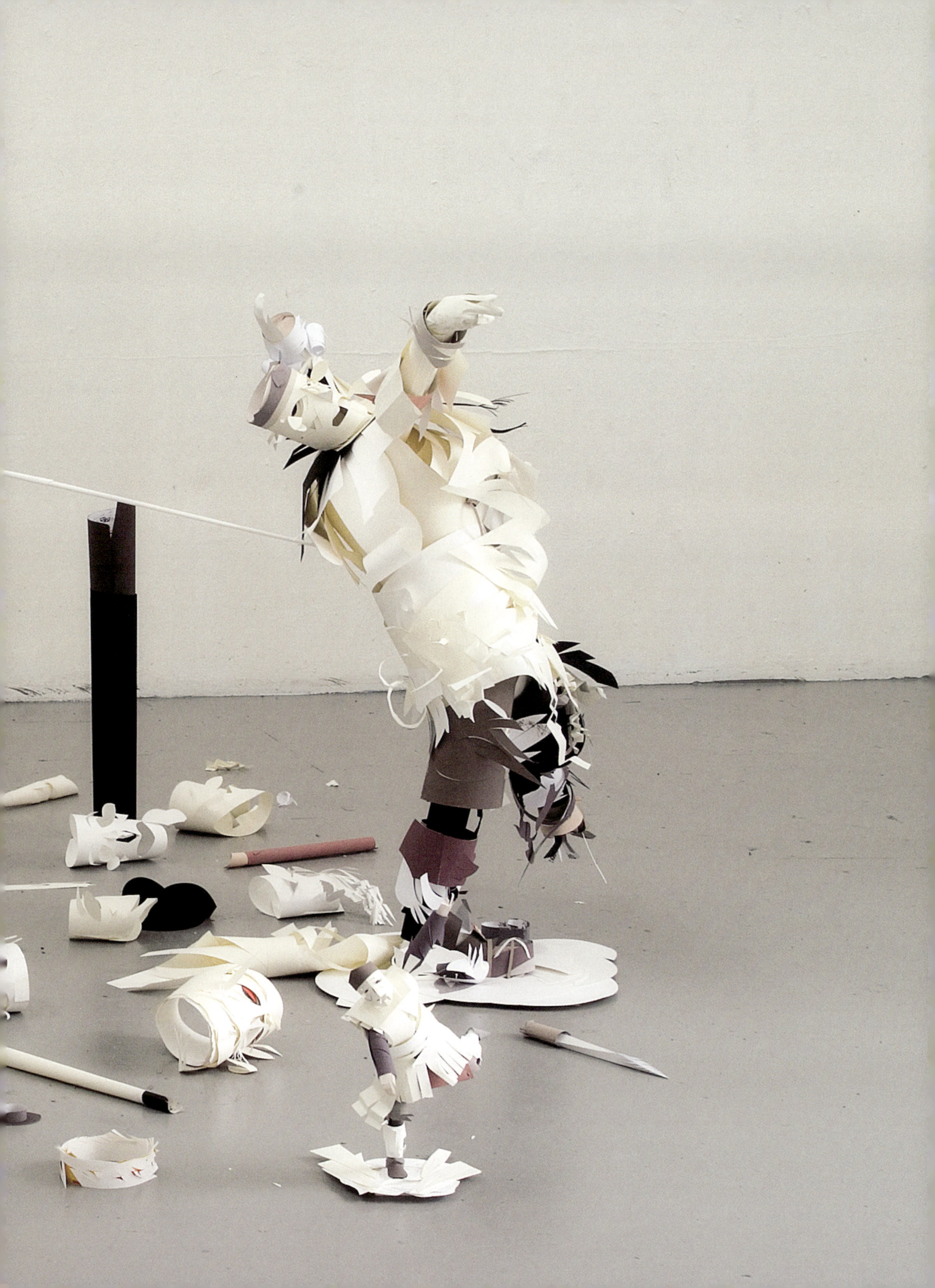

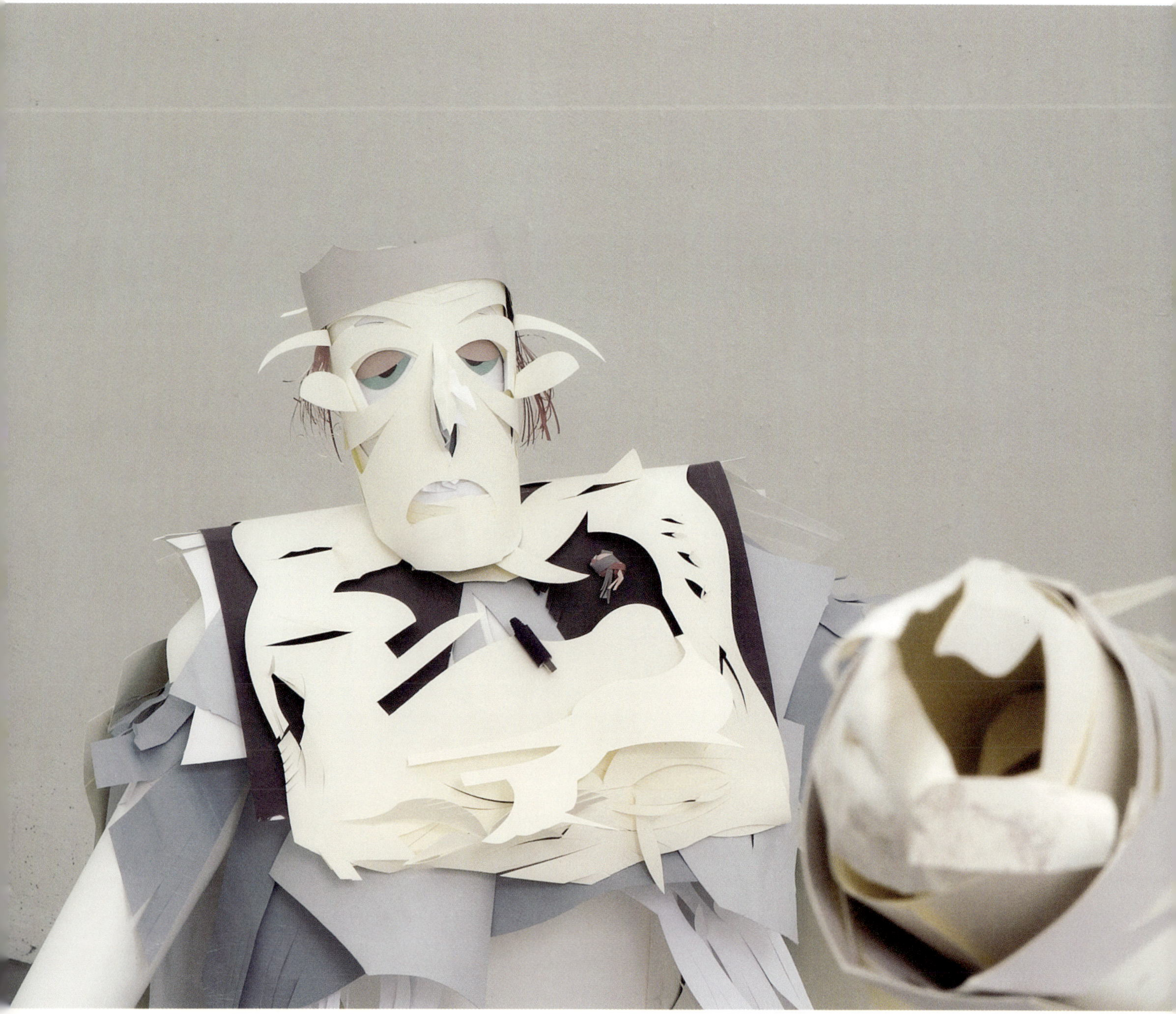

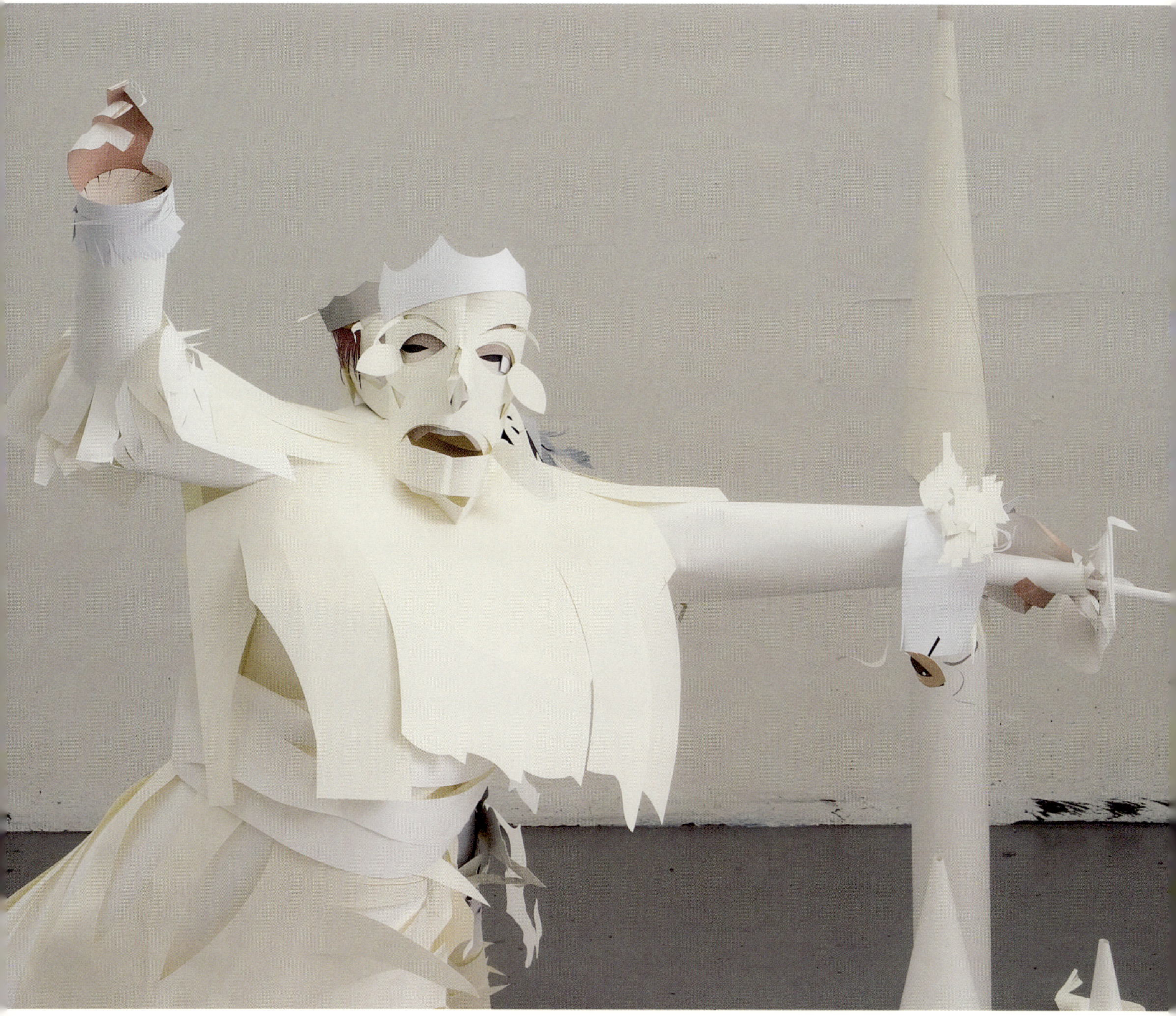

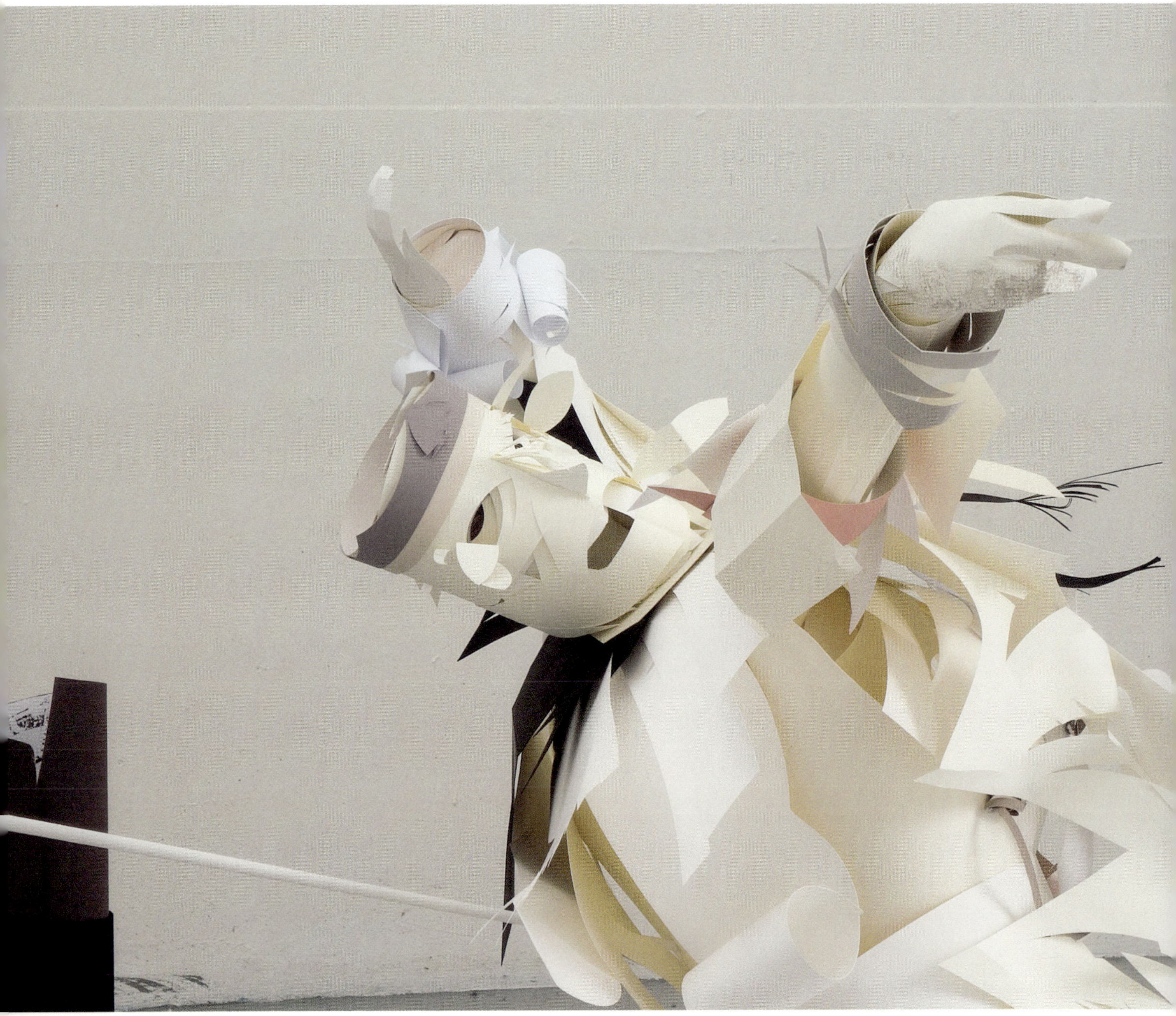

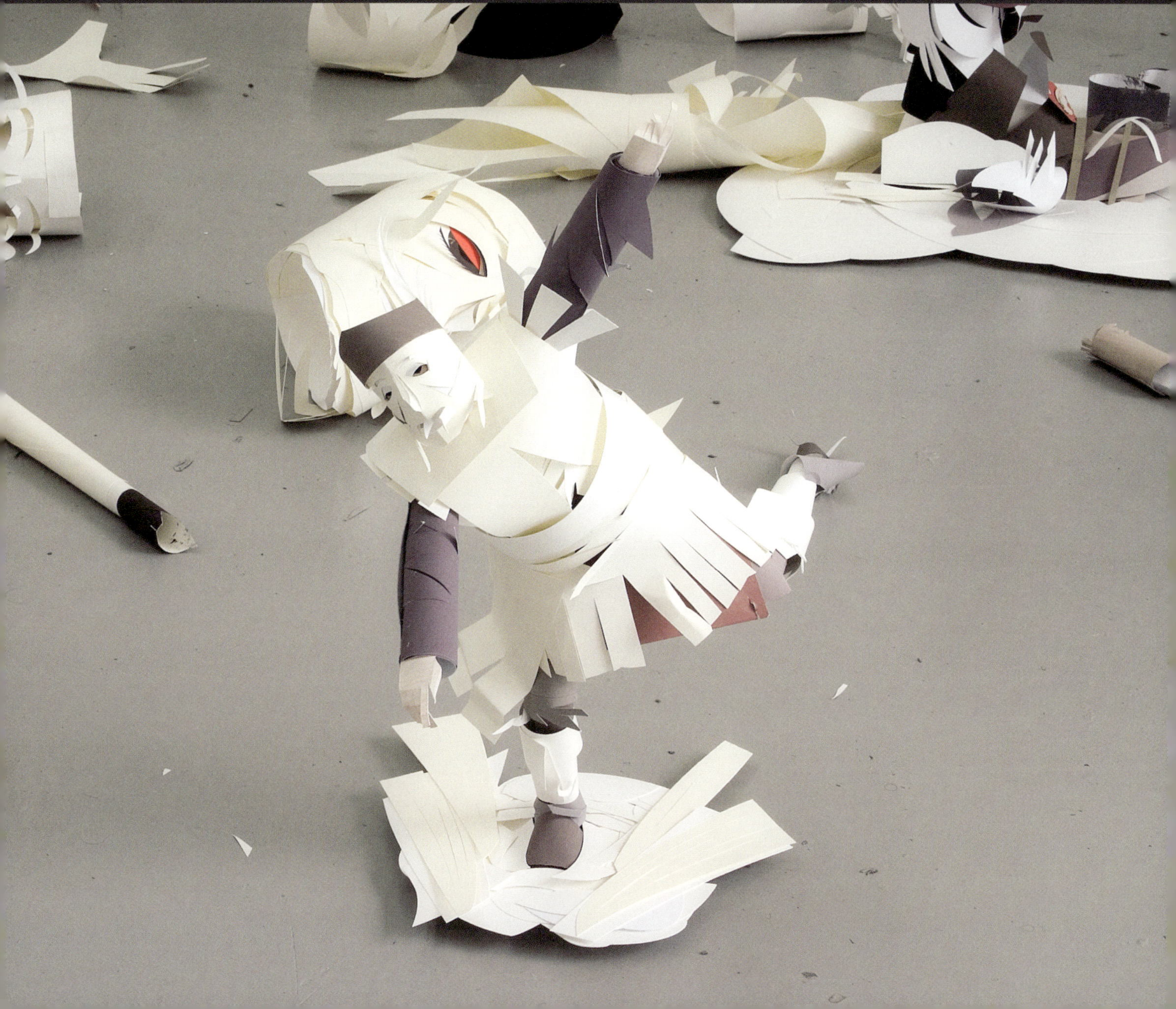

WHERE WERE YOU

2008 / INSTALLATION / WOOD / IRON / PAPER
110 X 130 X 95 CM

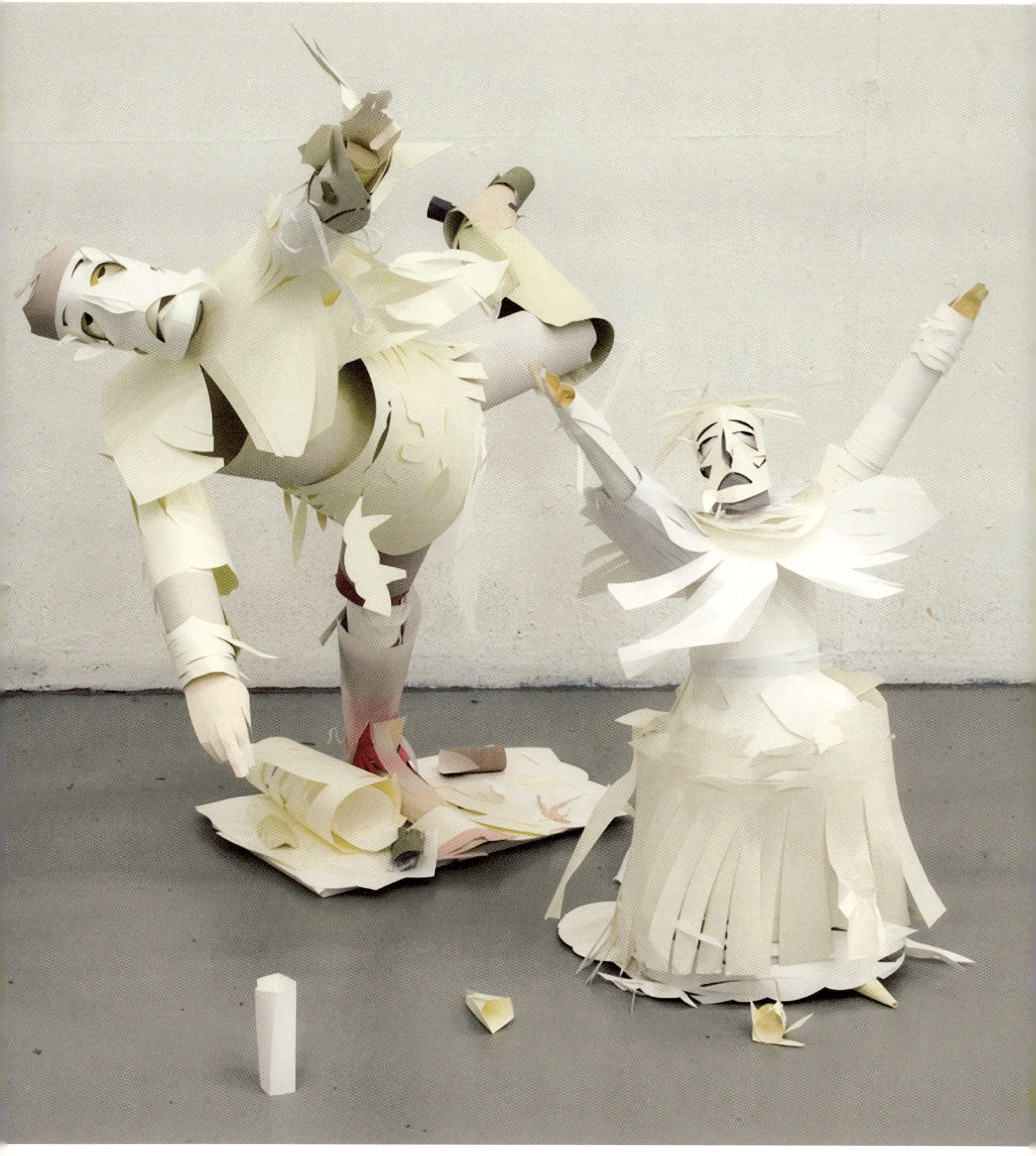

SUSHI AND THE KING

2008 / INSTALLATION / WOOD / IRON / PAPER
105 X 65 X 54 CM

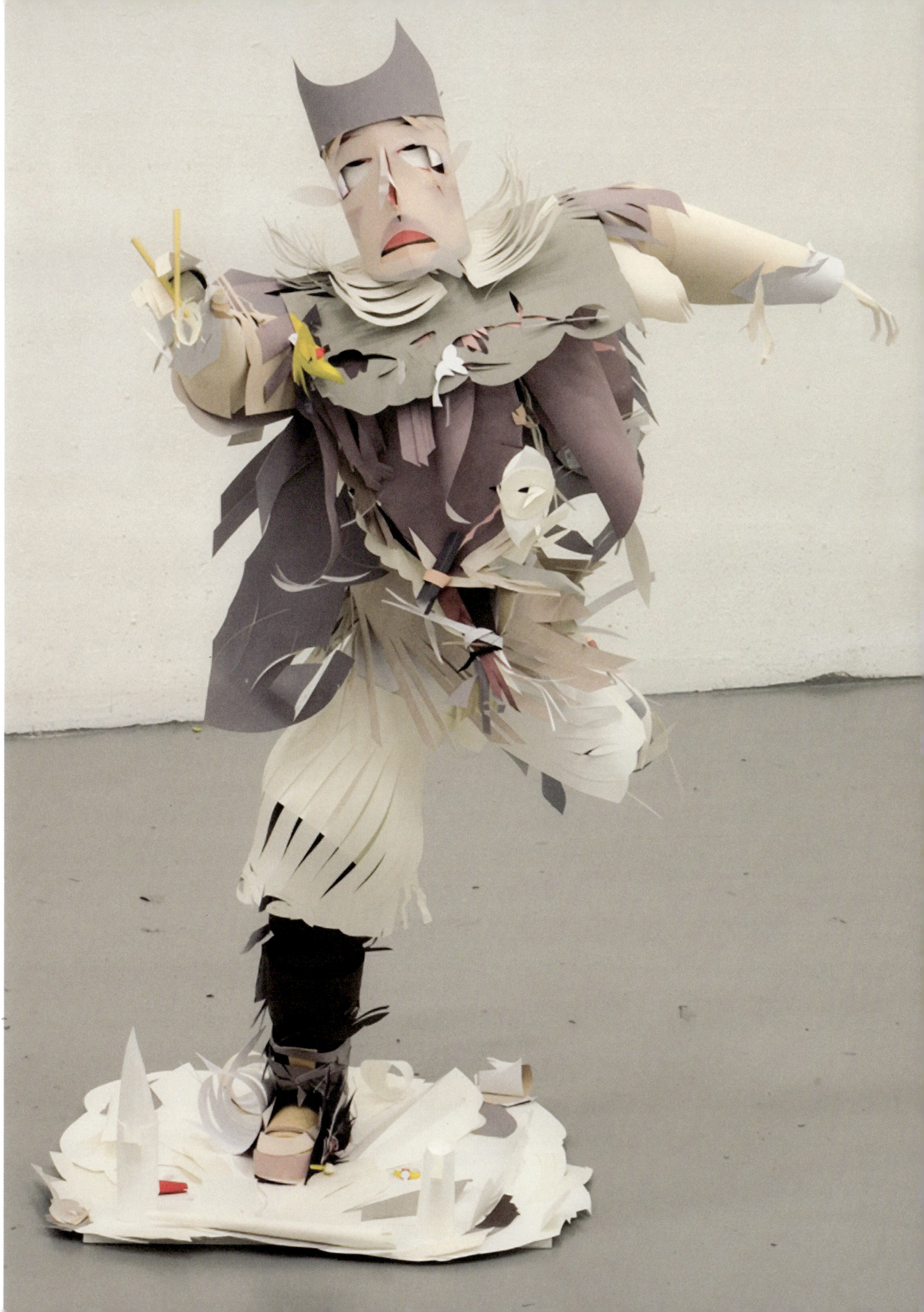

LET ME SWEEP THE DECORATIVE GODS,
AND DECORATIVE TRUTHS

2007 / INSTALLATION / WOOD / IRON / CLAY / PAPER
190 X 240 X 250 CM

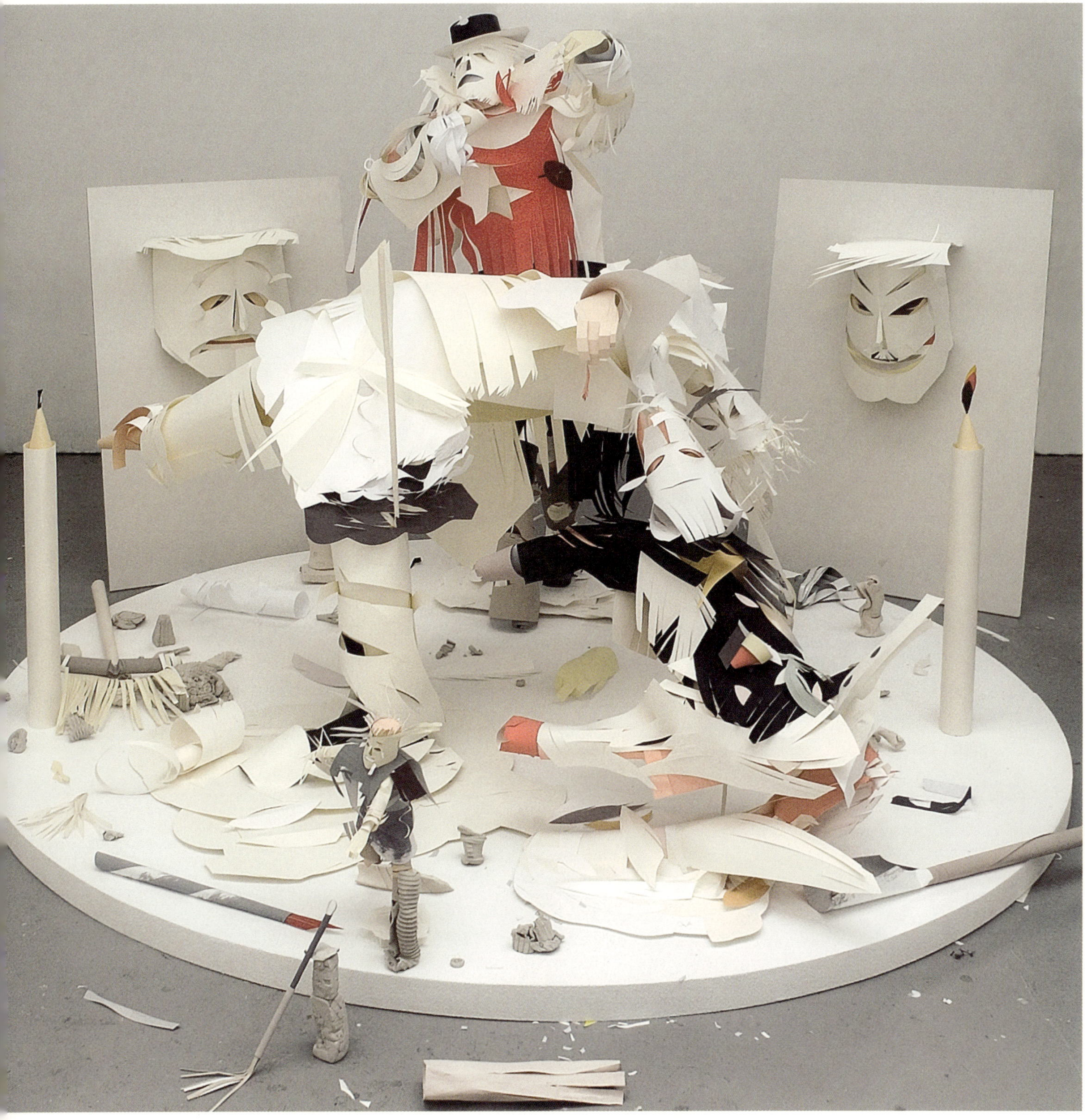

LEAVE ME ALONE,
CUT YOURSELF

2007 / INSTALLATION /
WOOD / IRON / CLAY / PAPER
210 X 340 X 230 CM

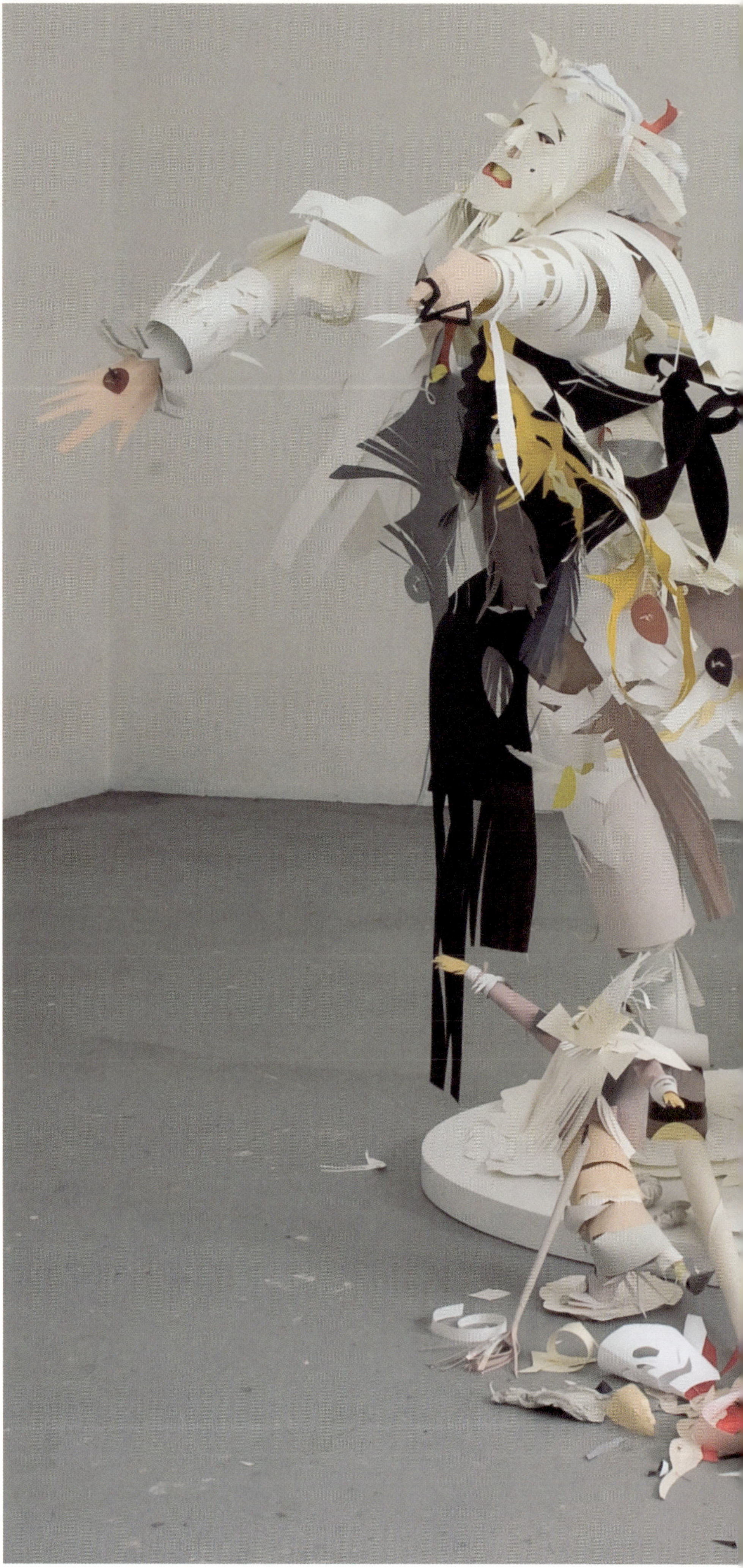

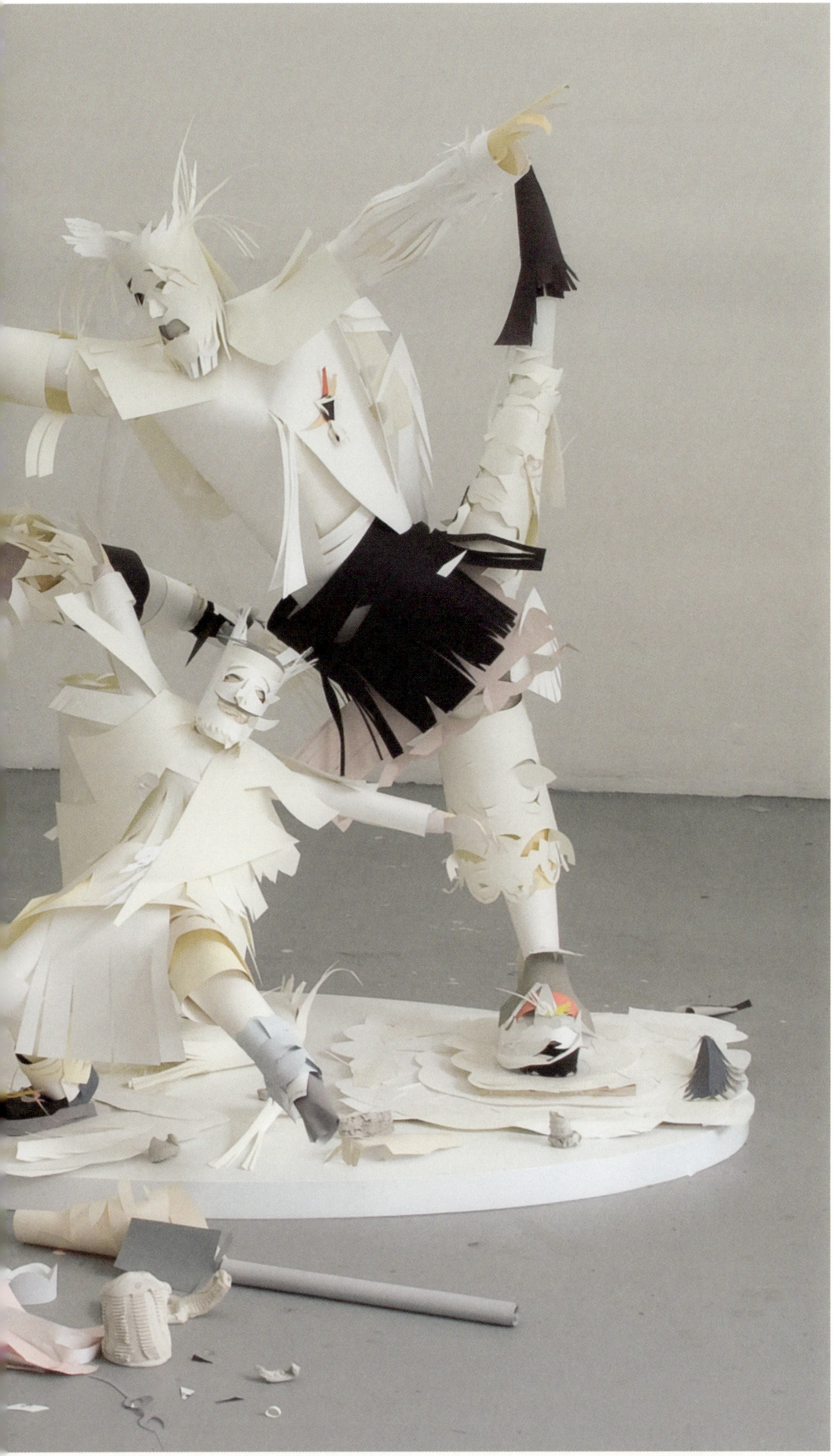

SHELTER

2007 / INSTALLATION / WOOD / IRON / PAPER
130 X 174 X 147 CM

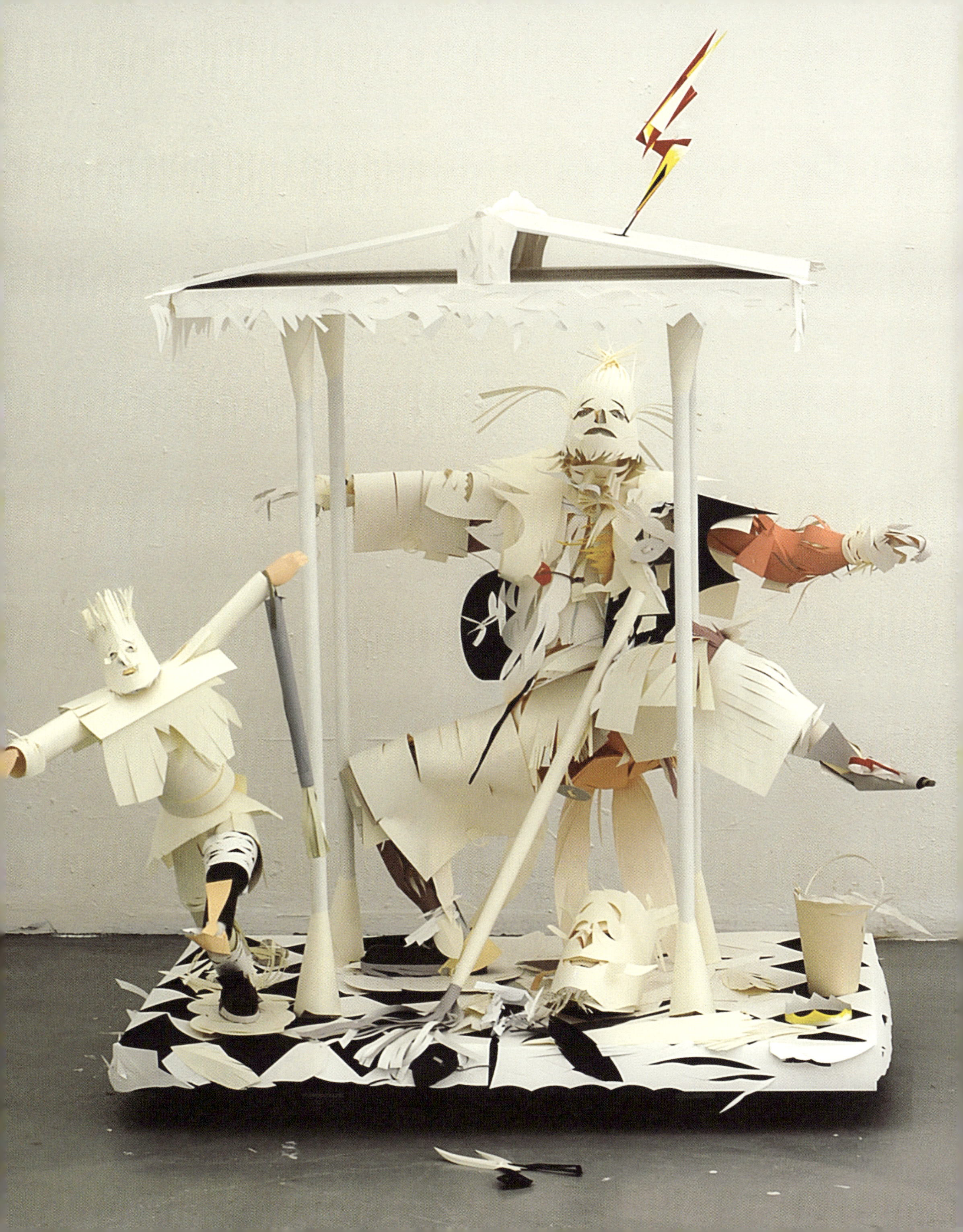

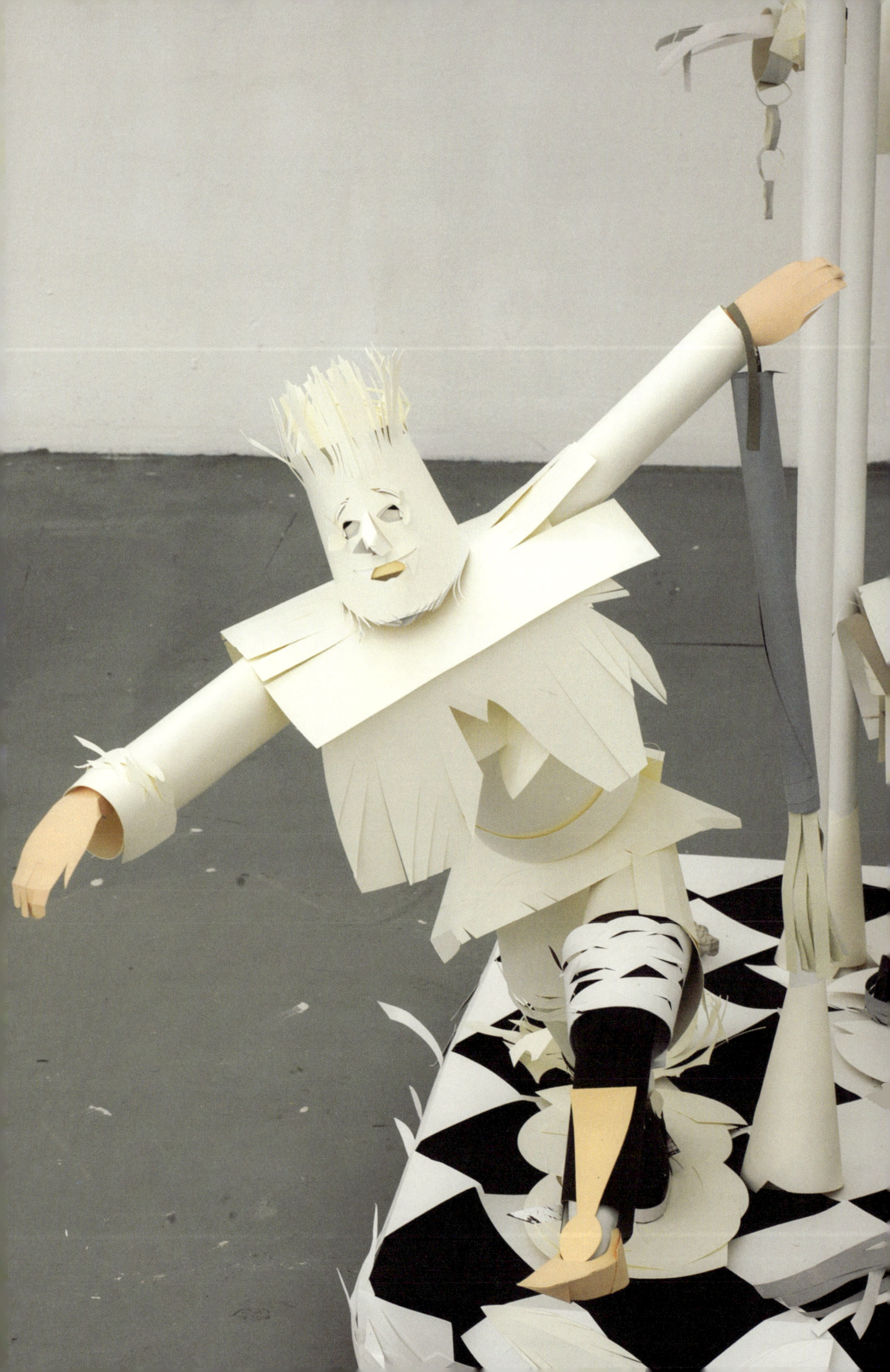

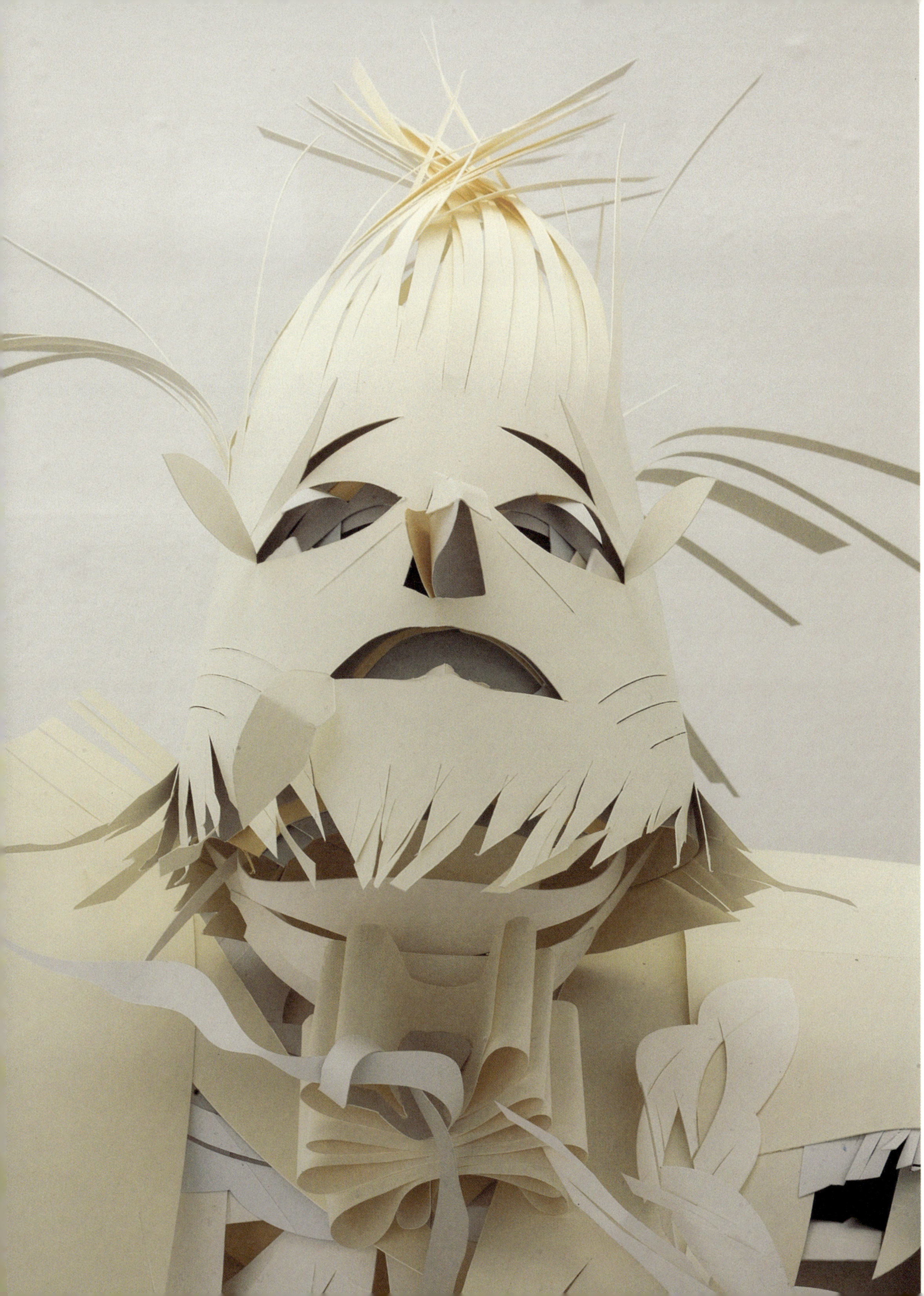

HUMAN BEHAVIOR

2007 / INSTALLATION / WOOD / IRON / CLAY /
PAPER / STIRRING SYSTEM / SOUND
170 X 310 X 200 CM

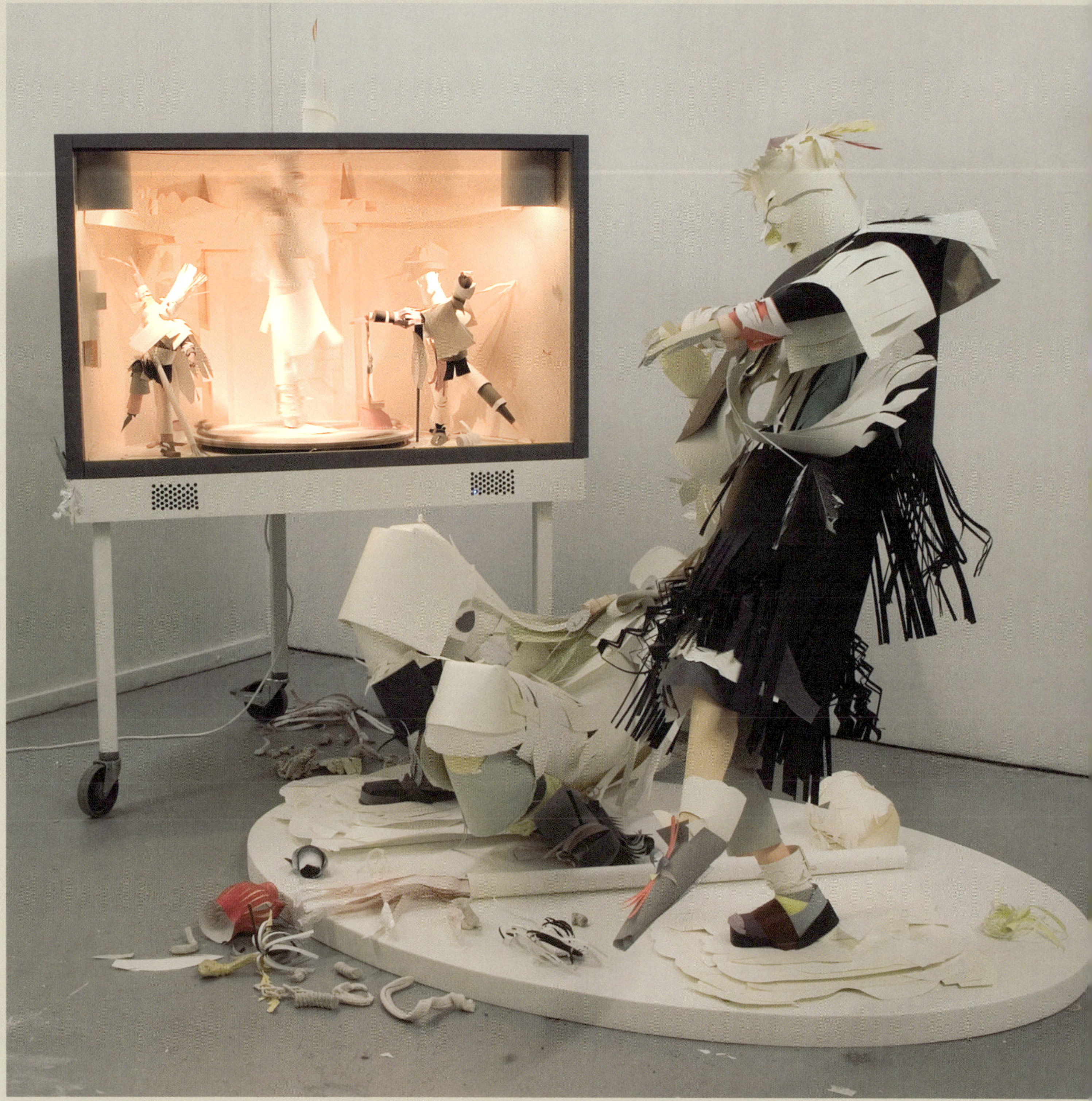

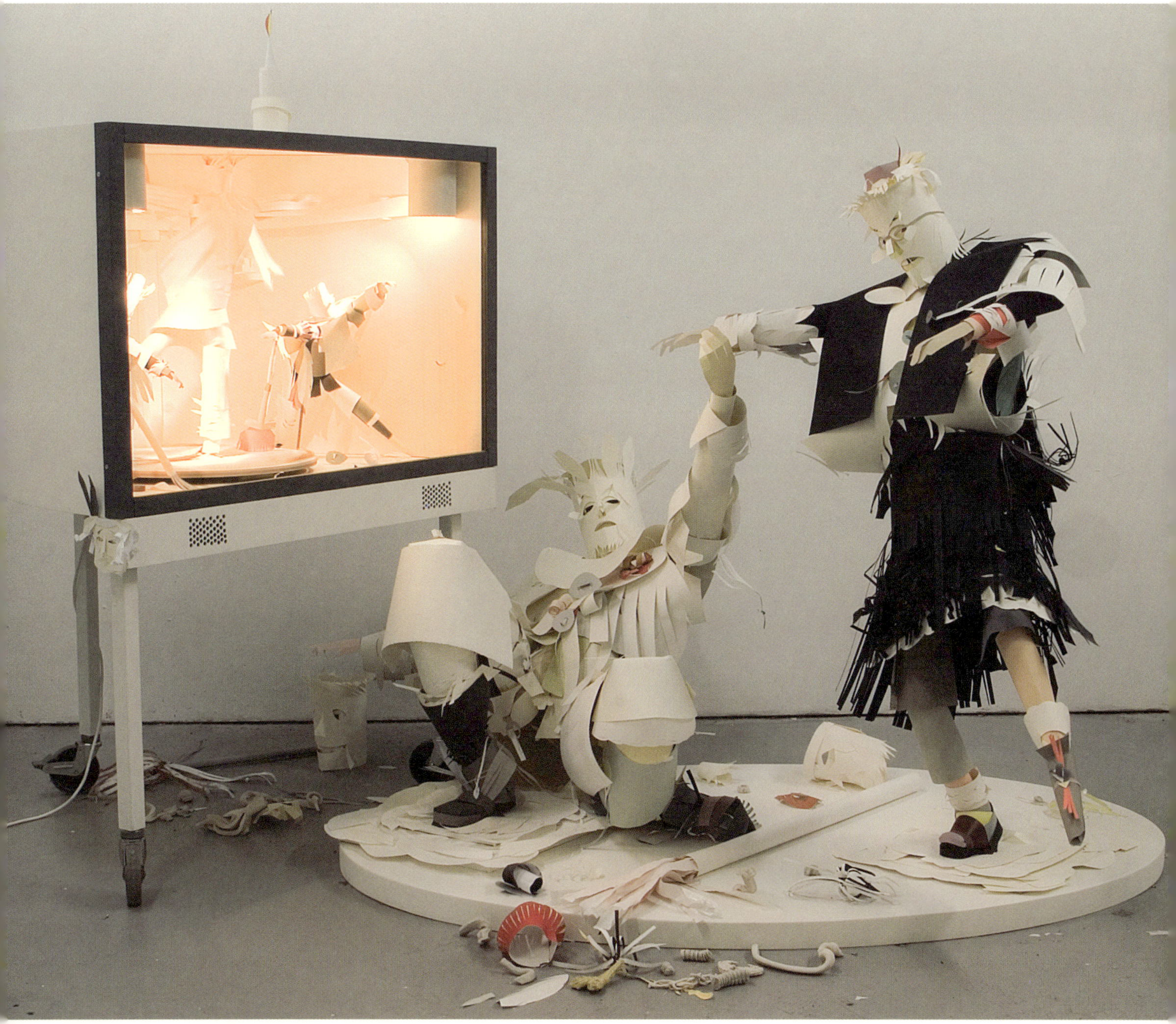

IN BETWEEN MOMENTS

2007 / INSTALLATION / WOOD /
IRON / CLAY / PAPER
195 X 230X 170 CM

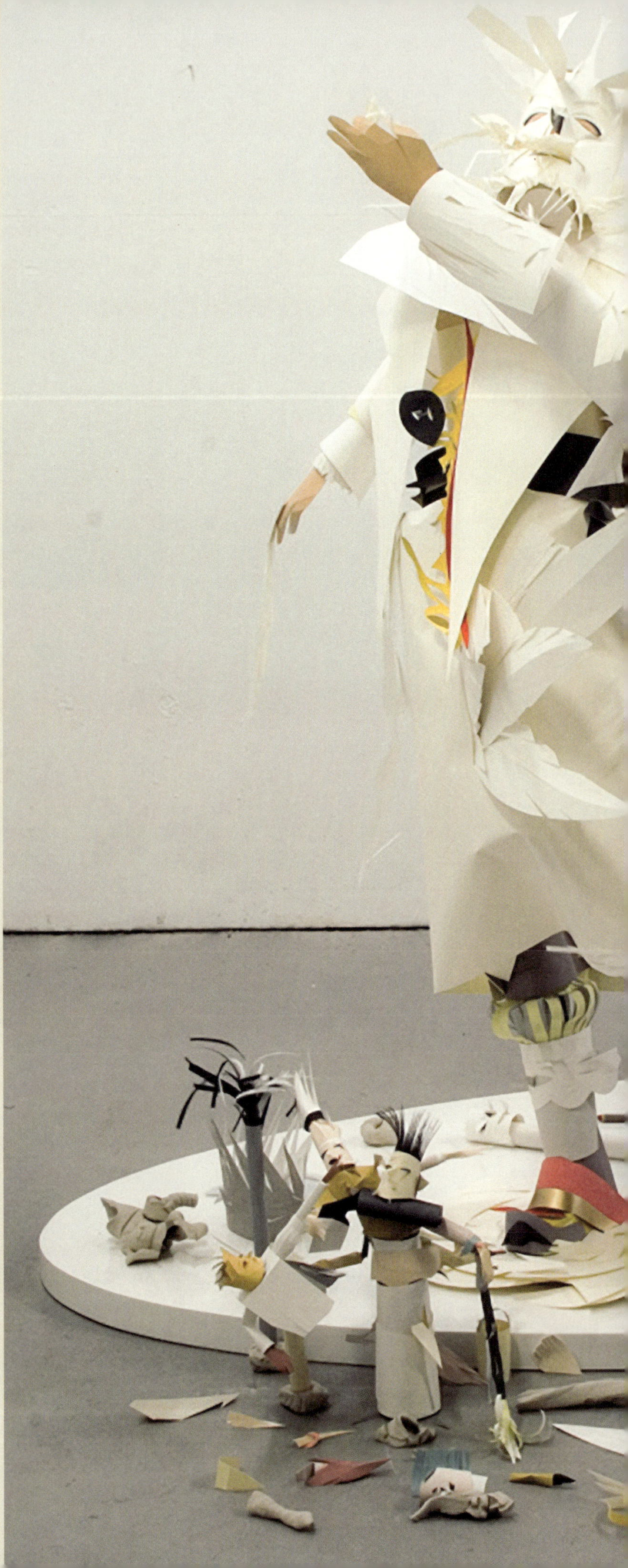

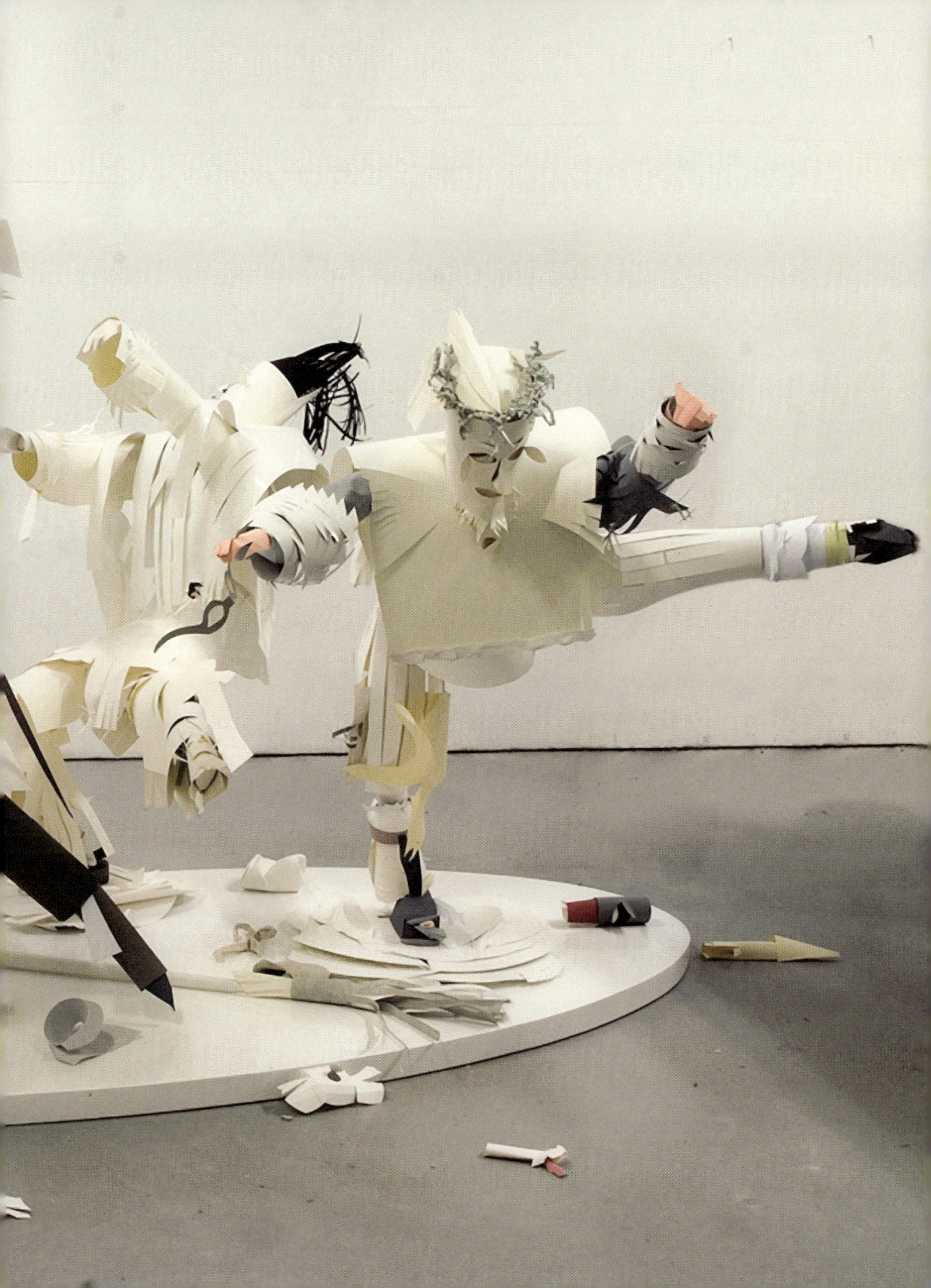

OUR GODS

2007 / INSTALLATION / WOOD / IRON / CLAY / PAPER
170 X 140 X 120 CM

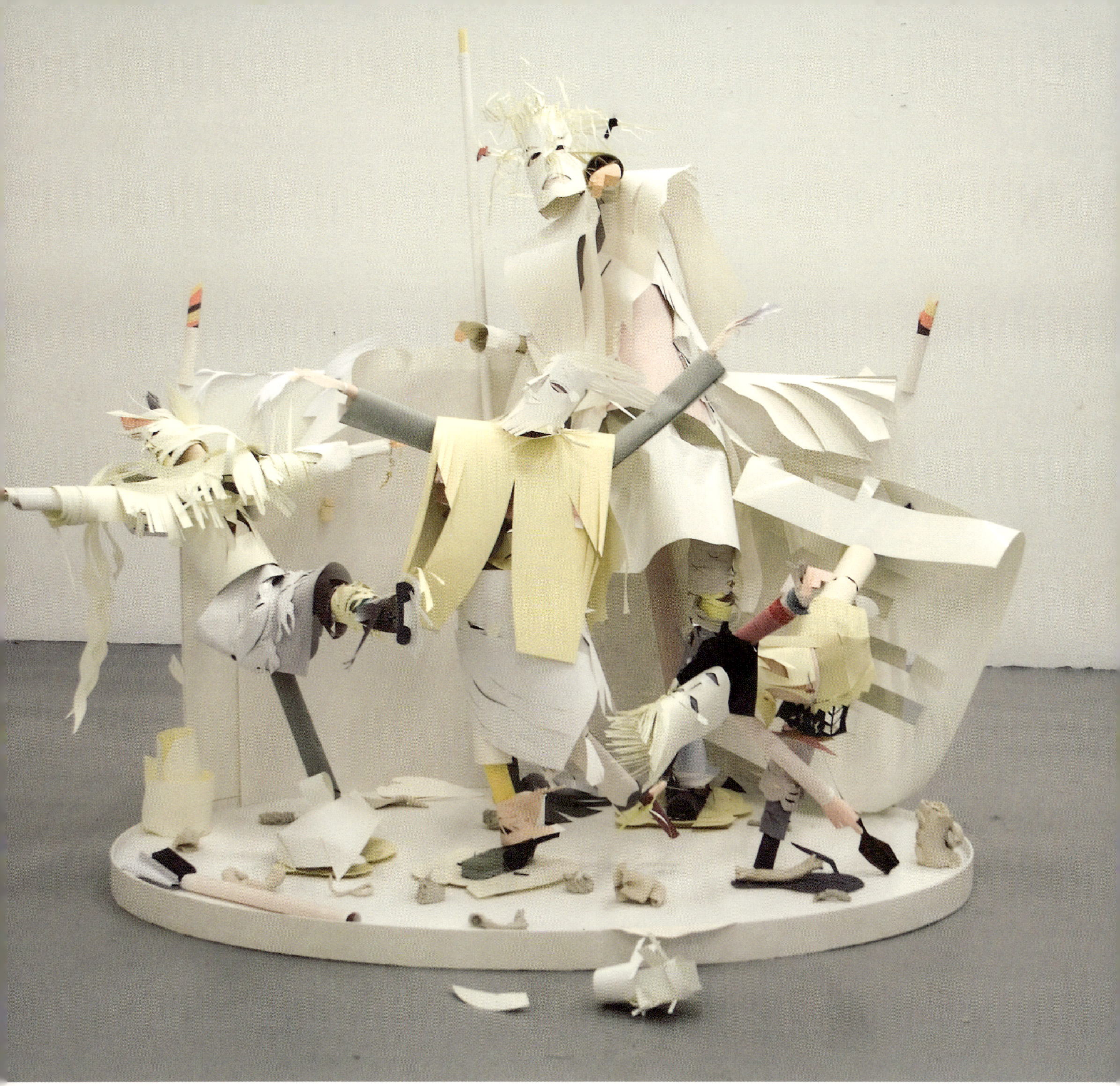

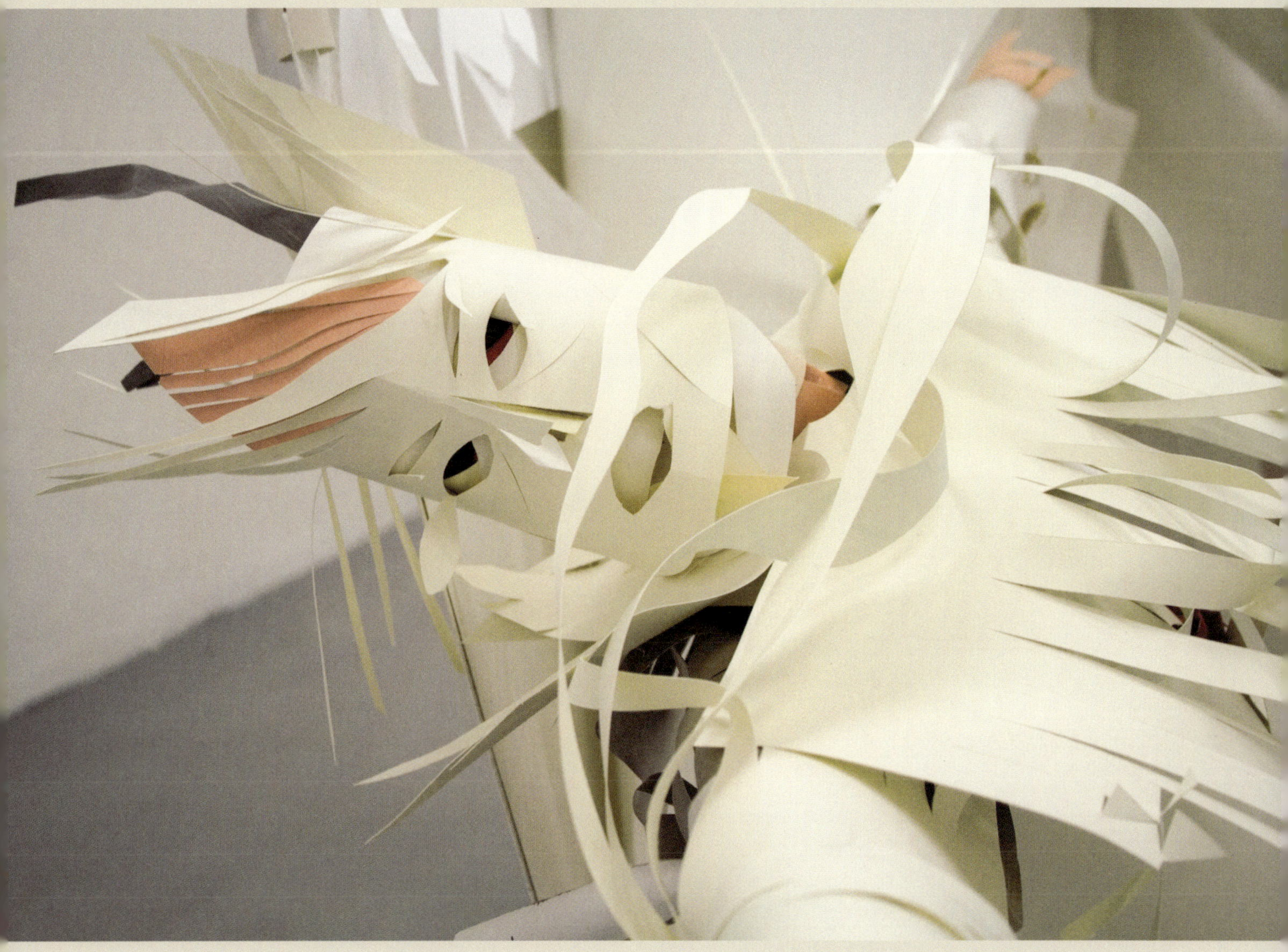

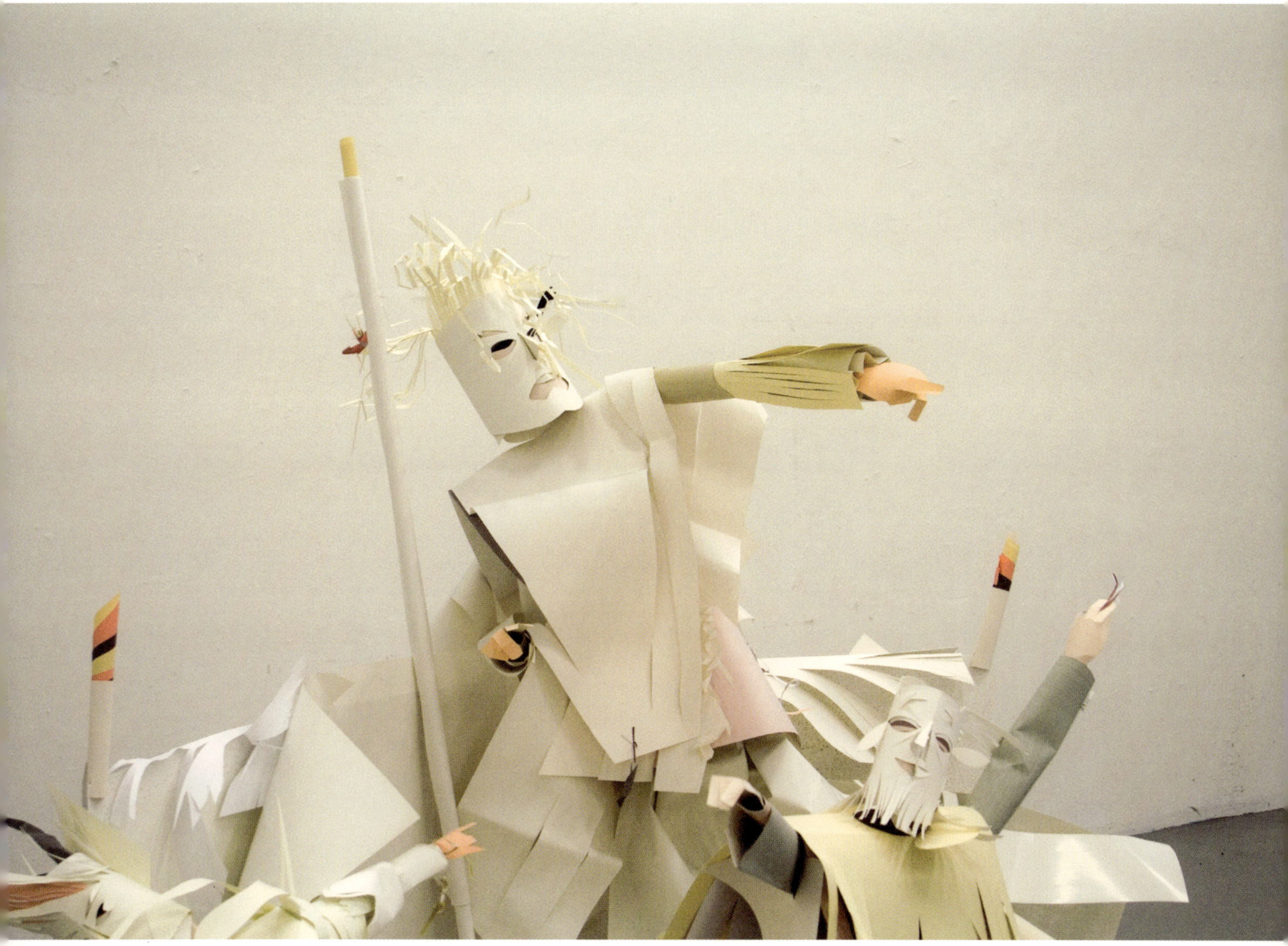

HISTORY OF A SECT, DON'T GO INSIDE,
DON'T TOUCH

2006 / INSTALLATION / WOOD / IRON / CLAY / PAPER
210 X 540 X 650 CM

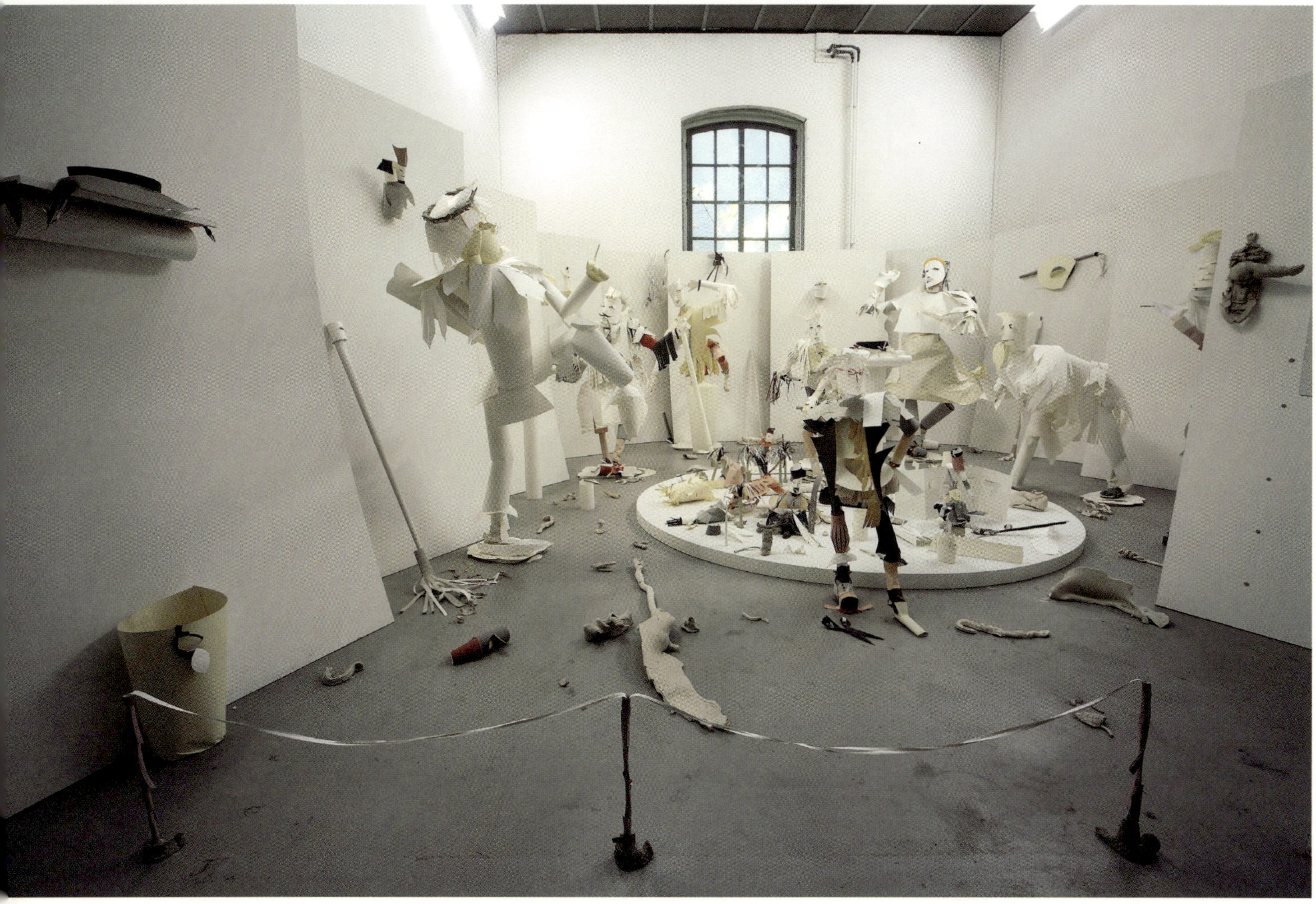

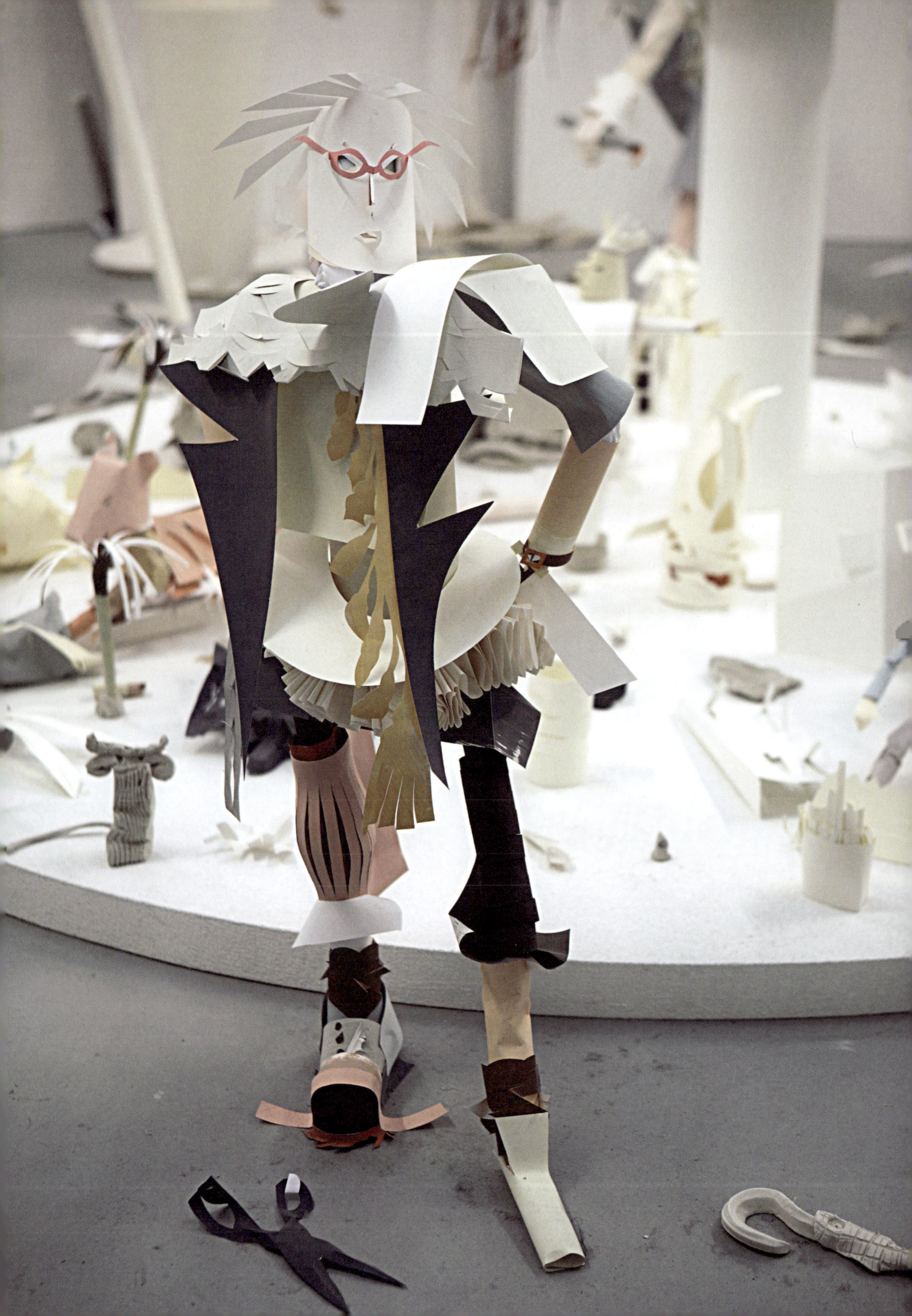

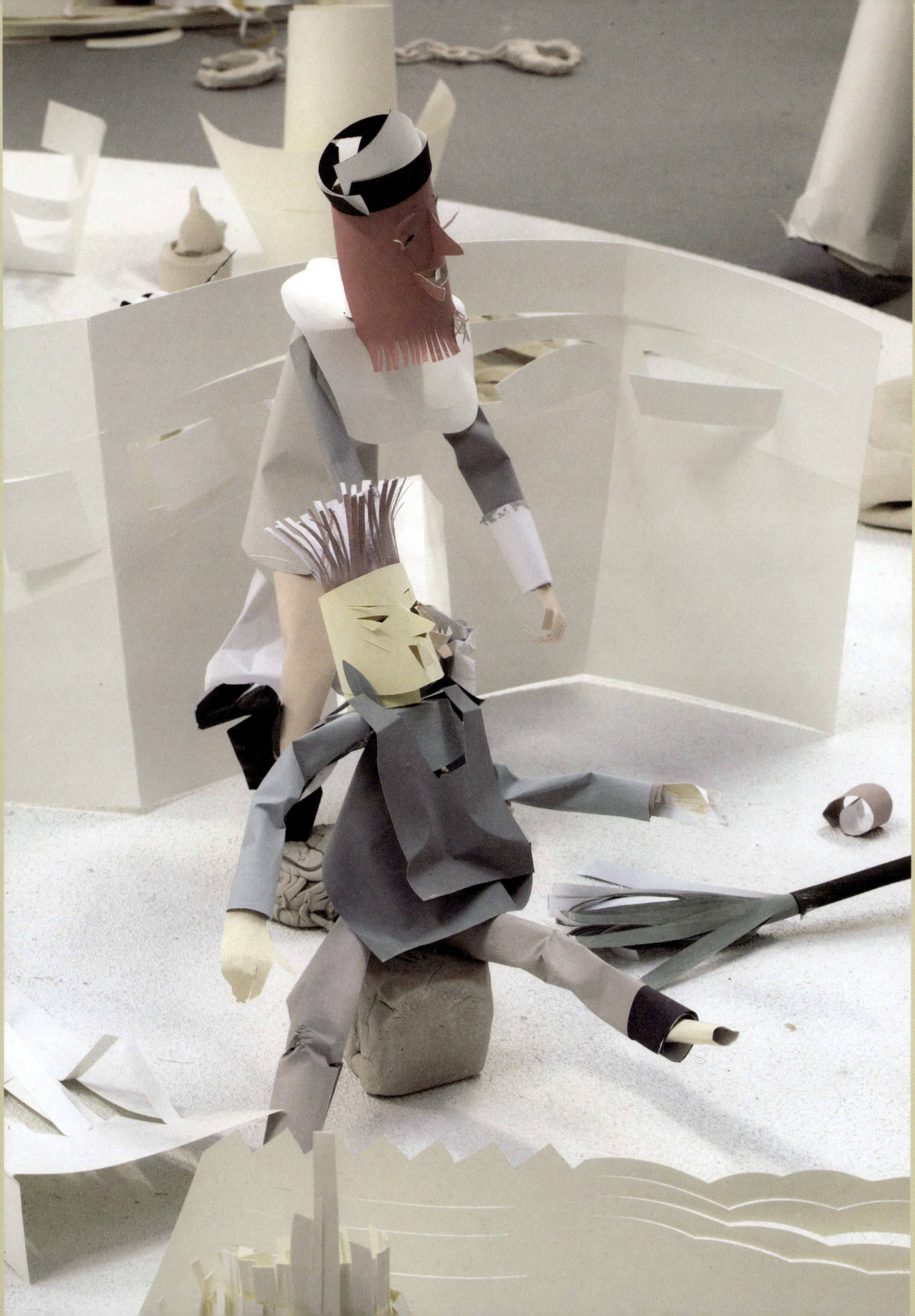

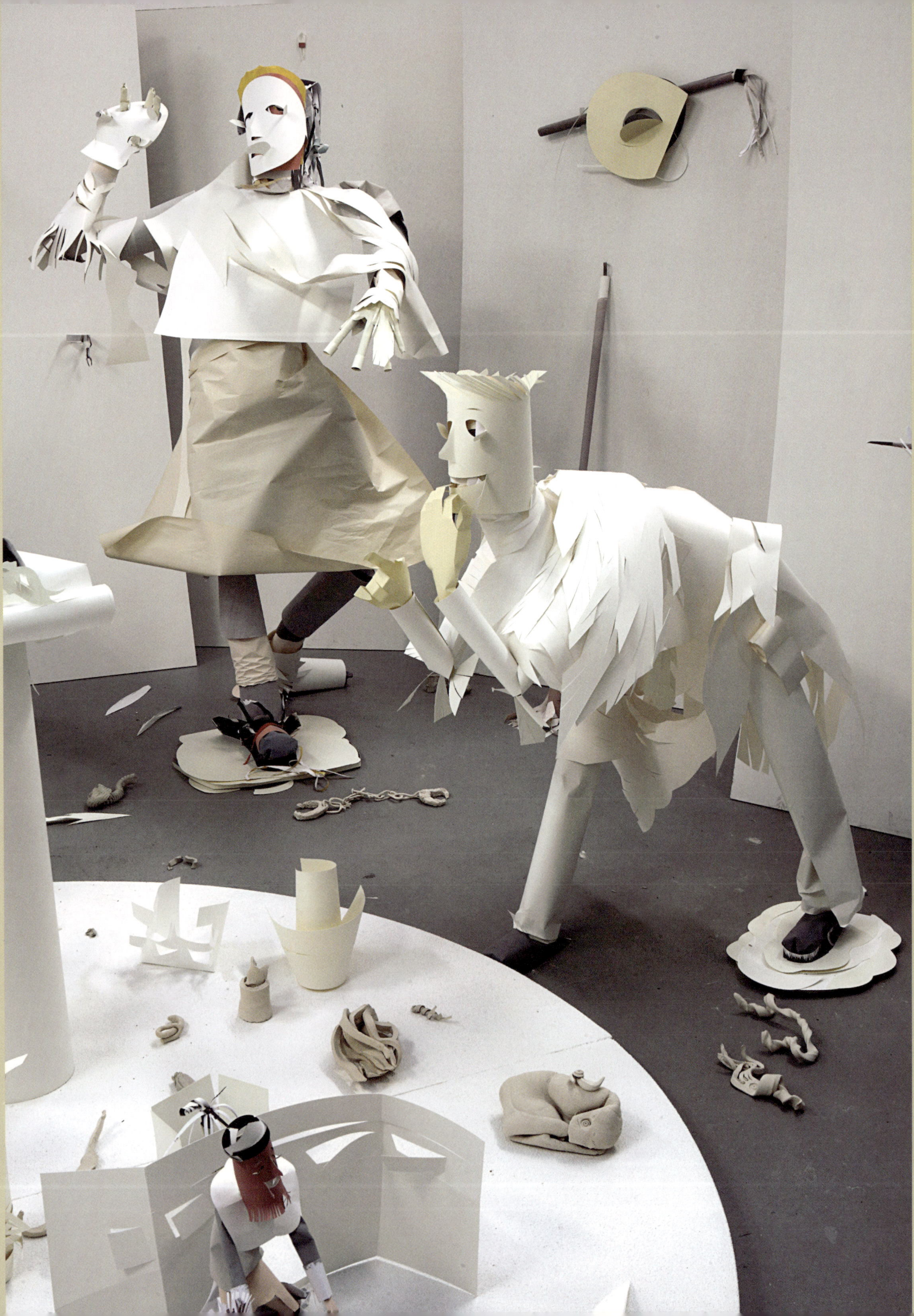

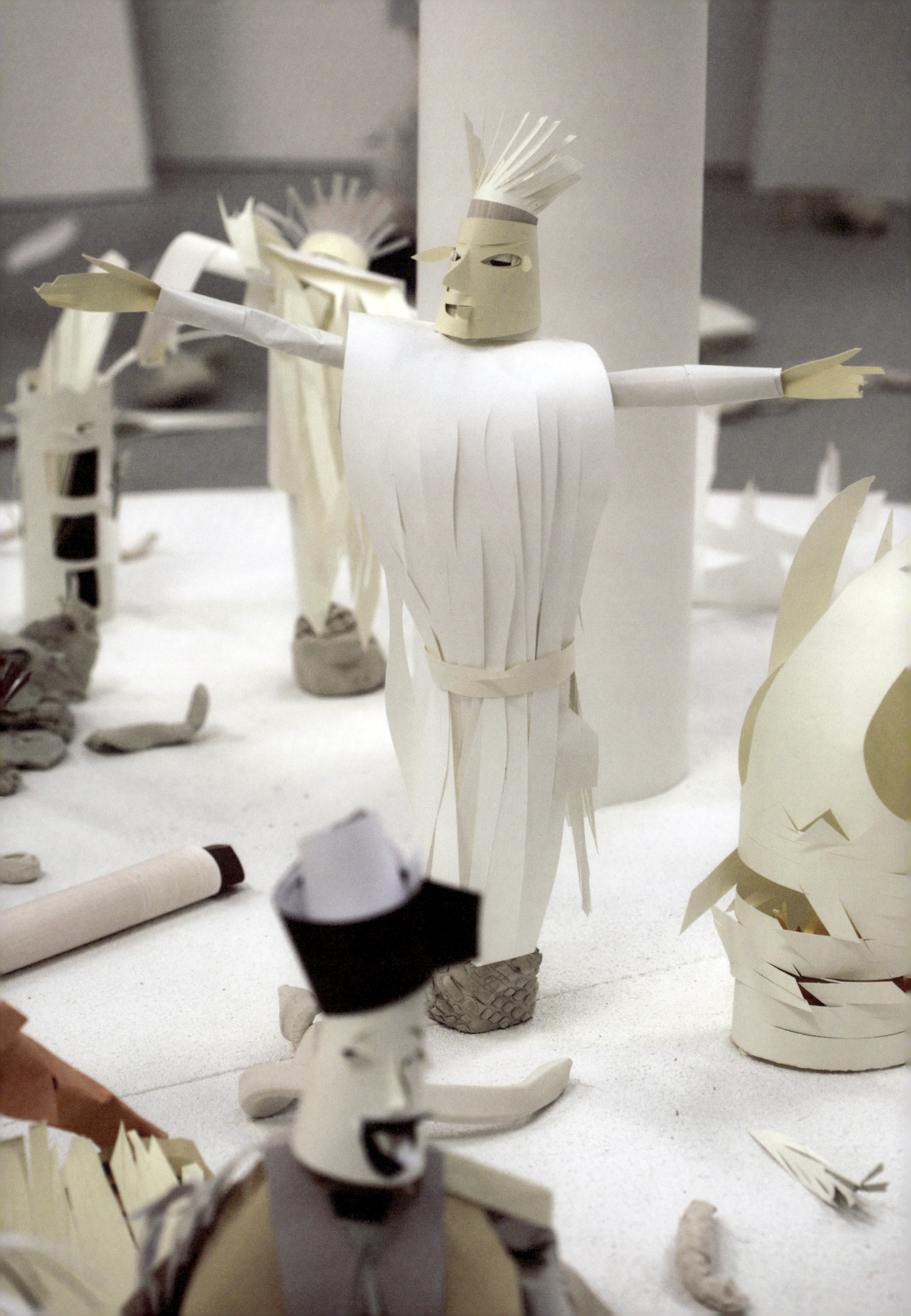

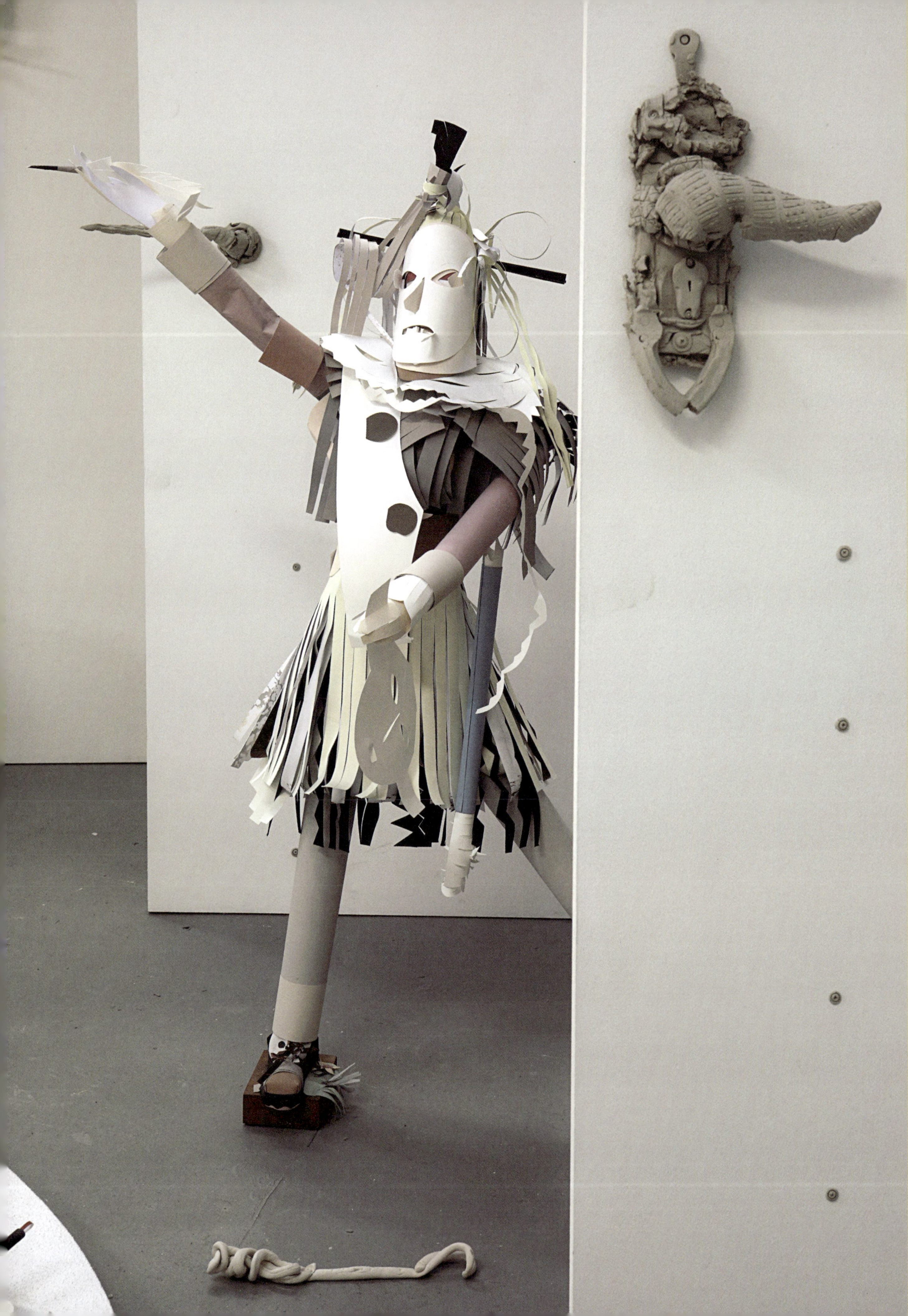

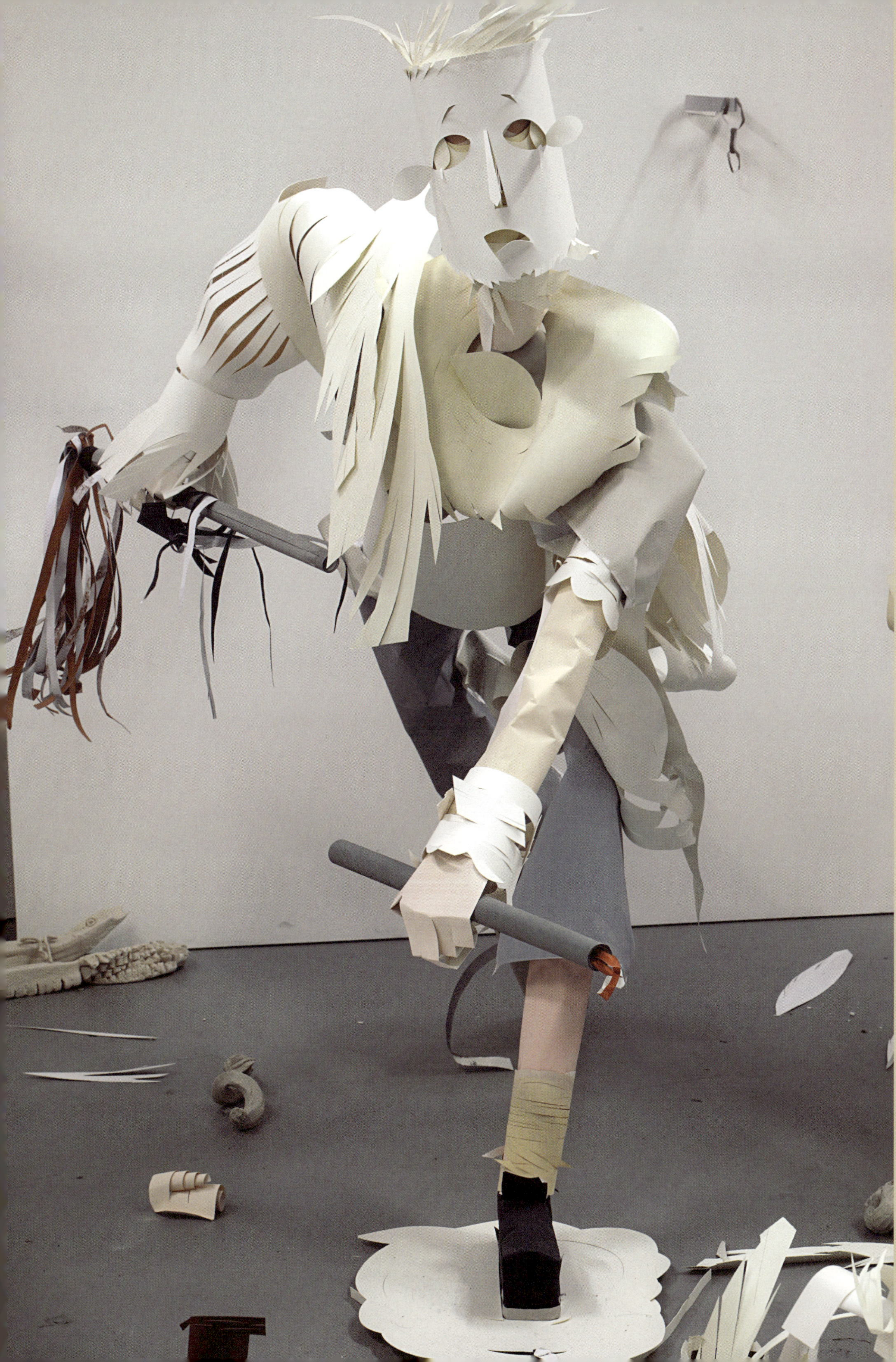

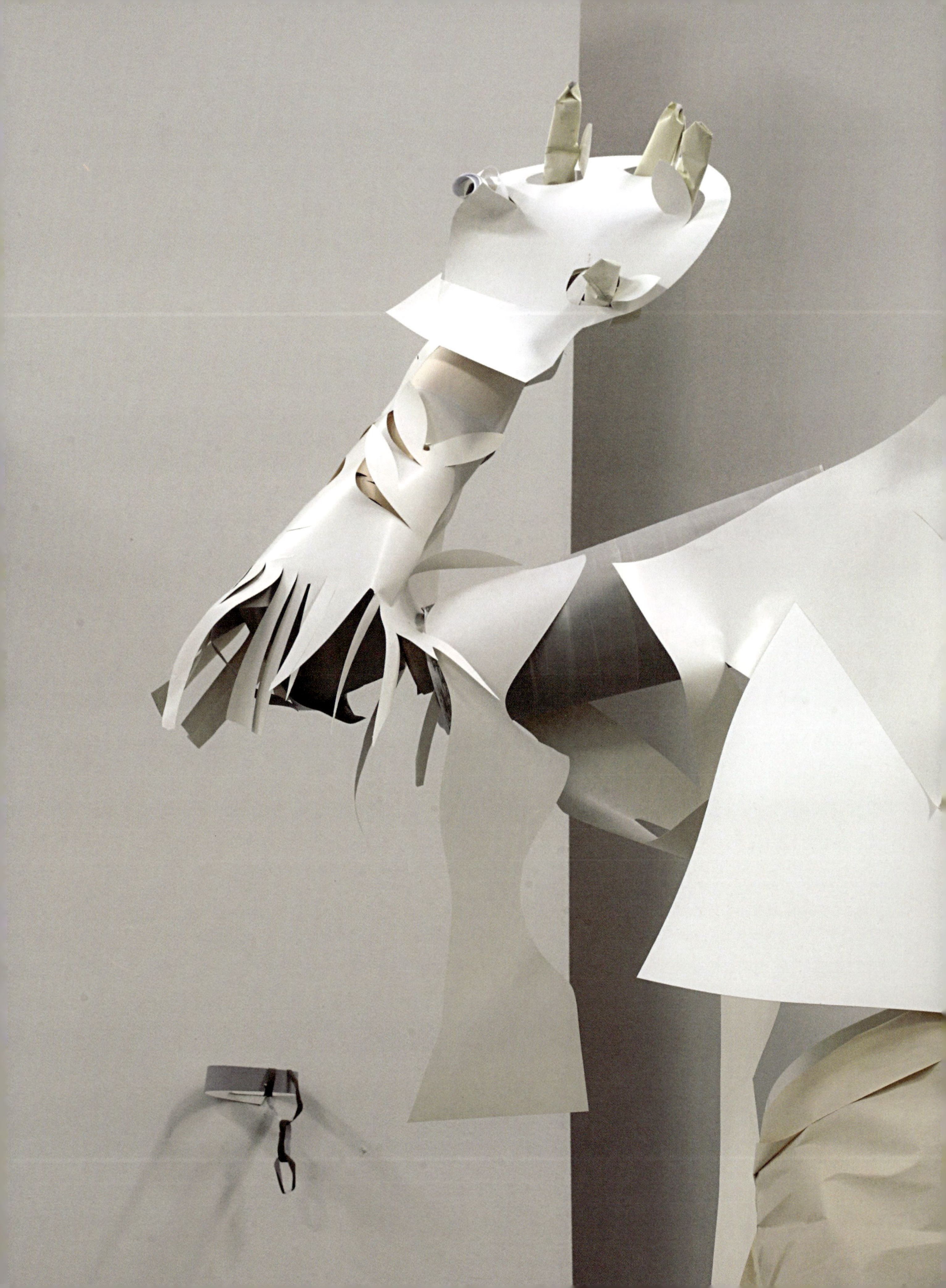

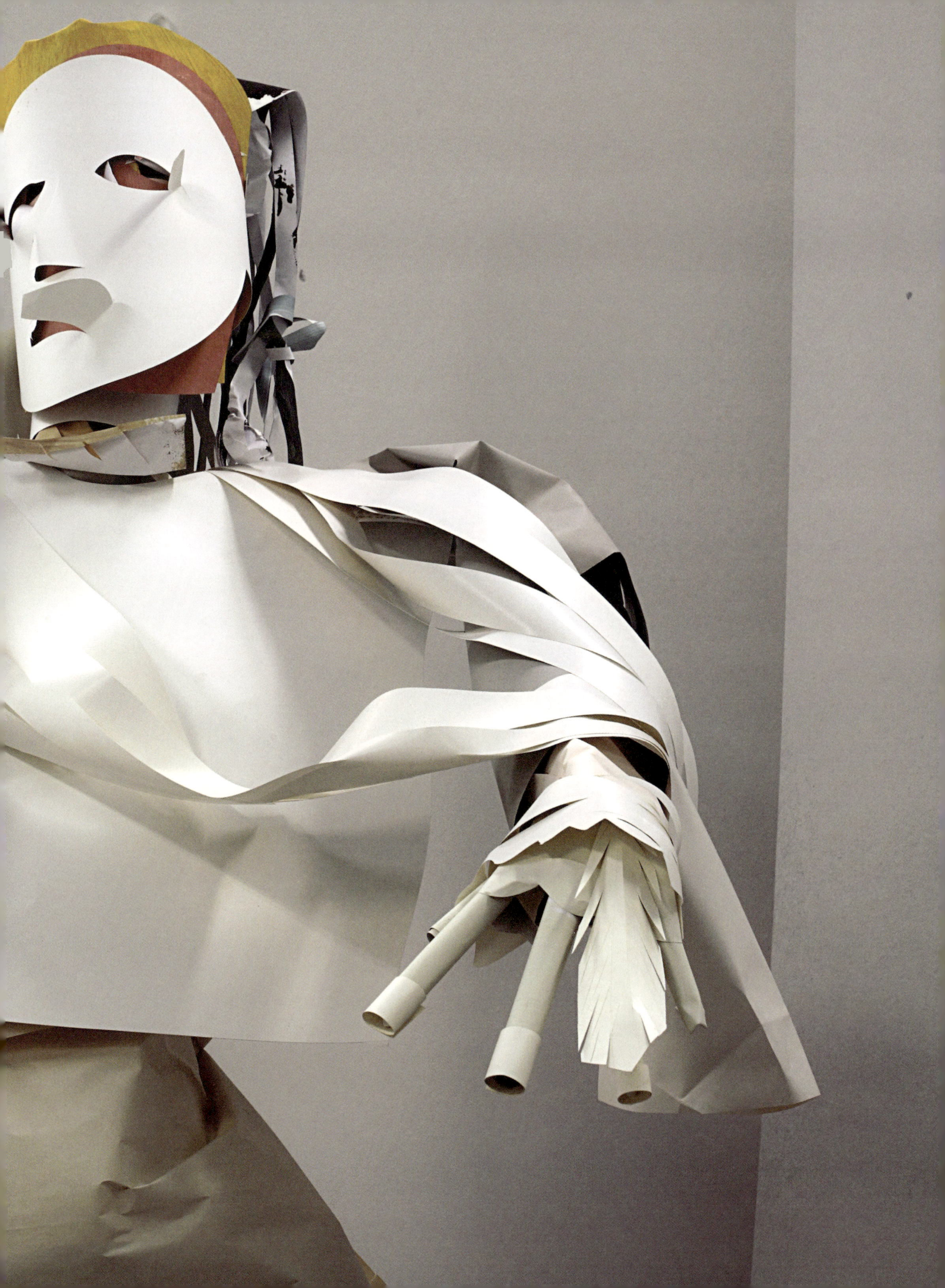

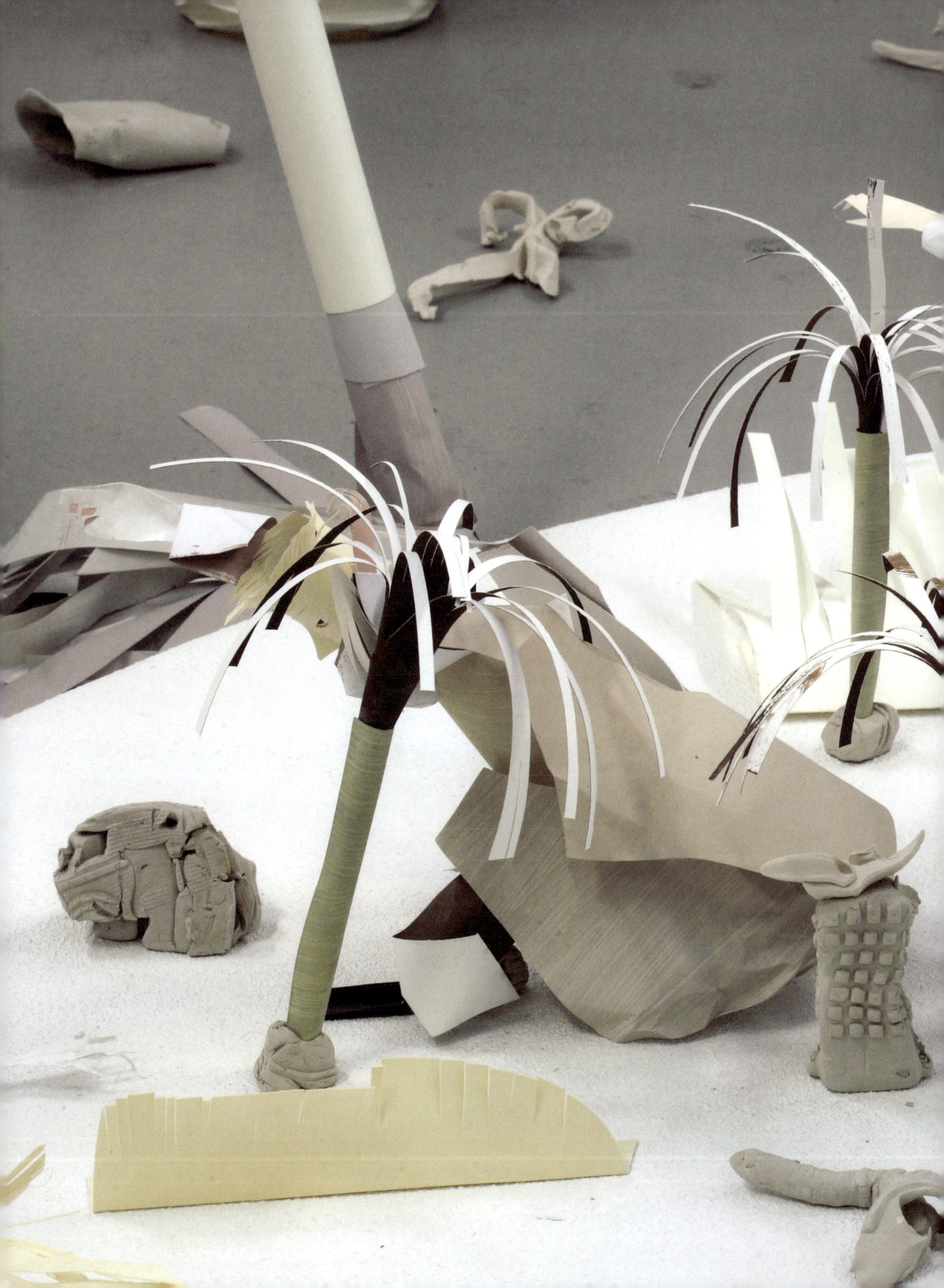

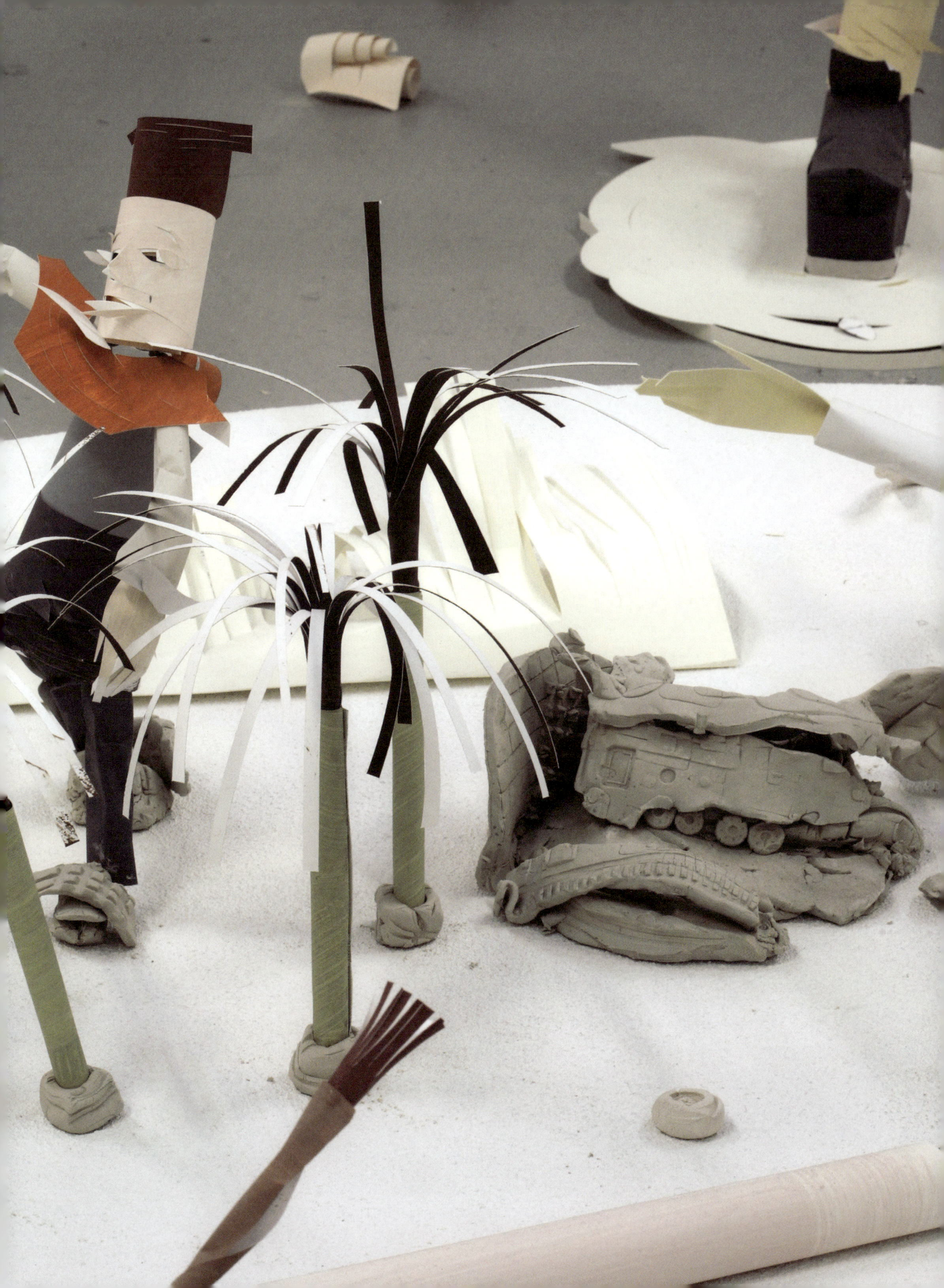

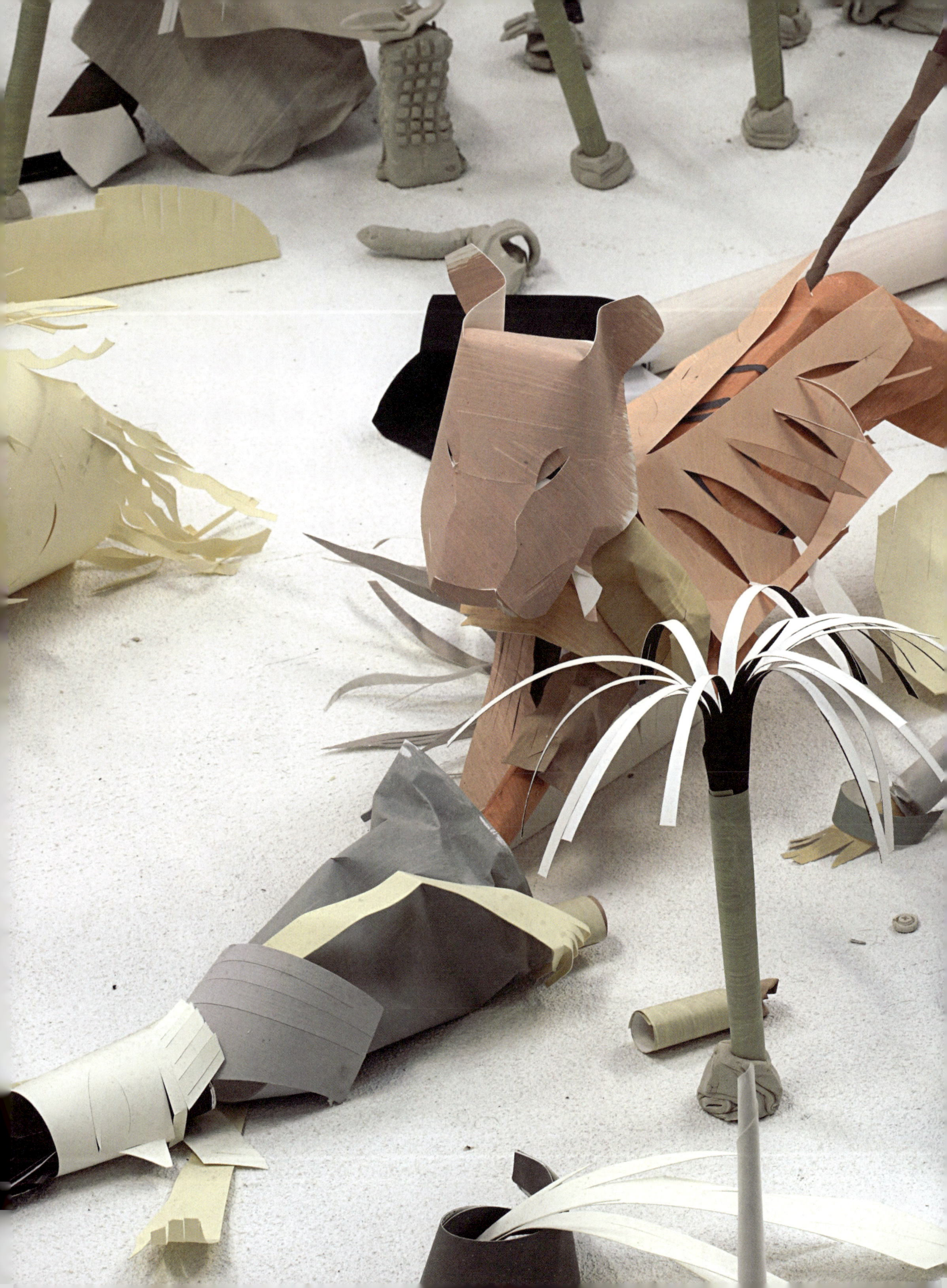

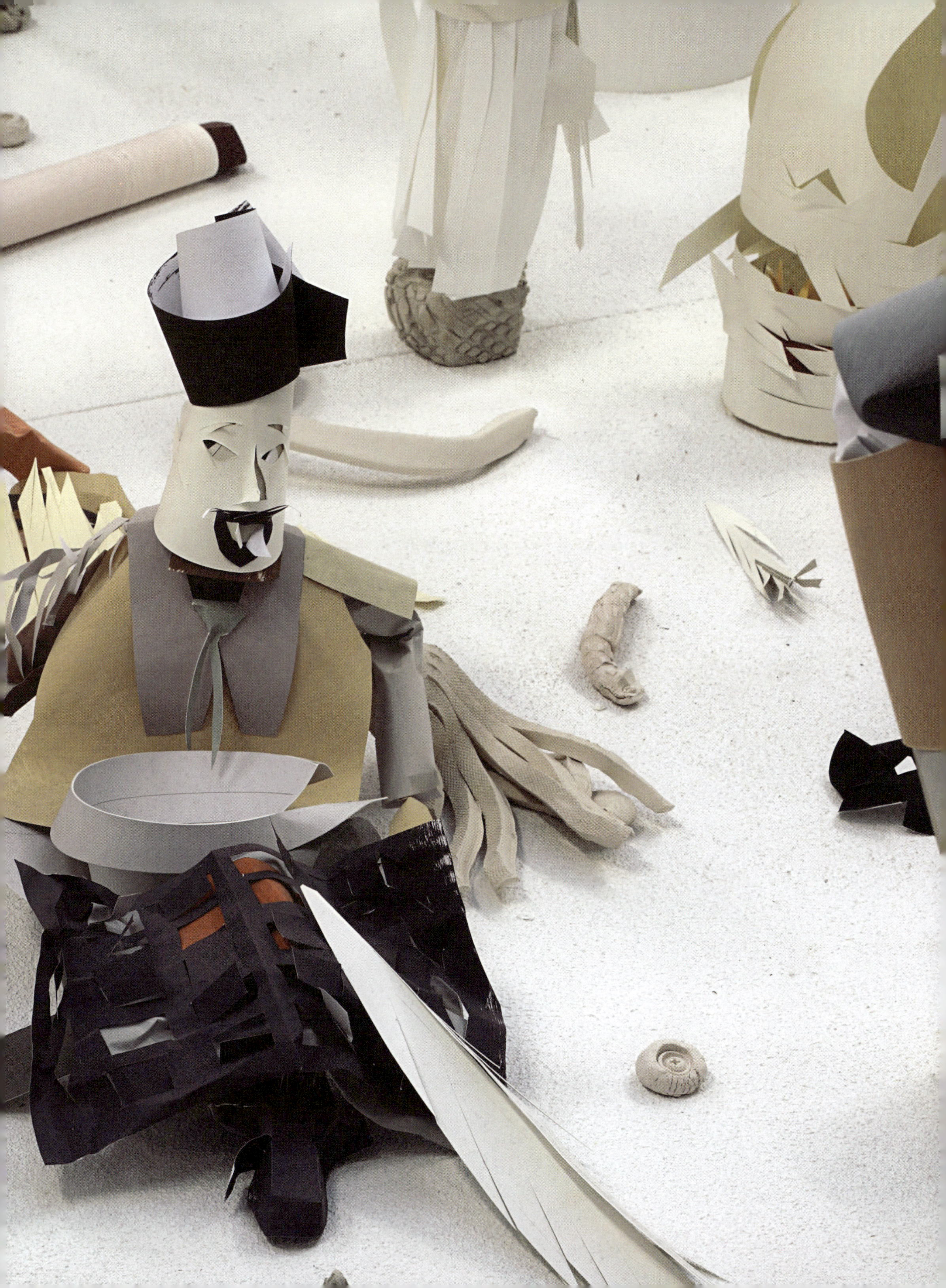

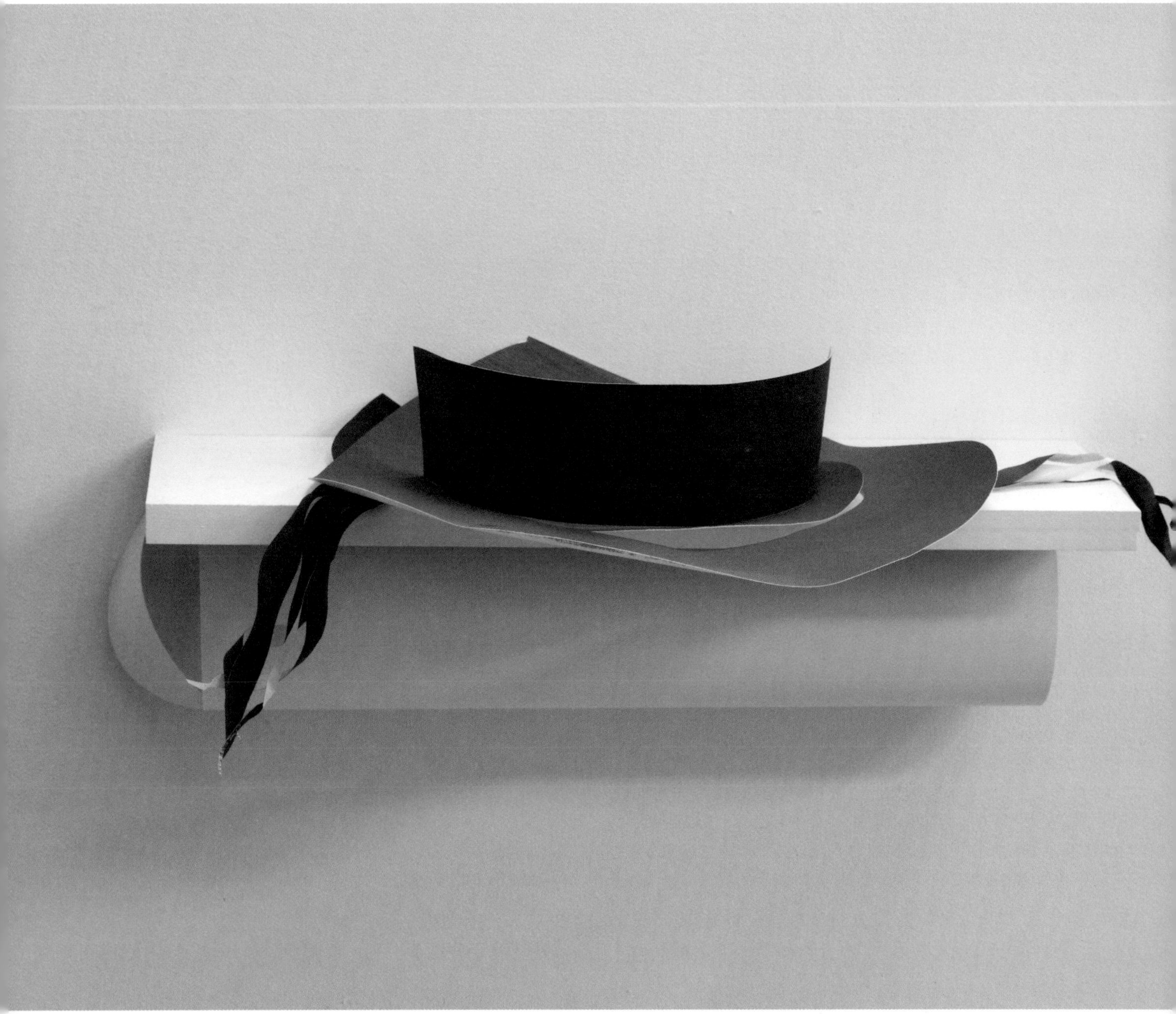

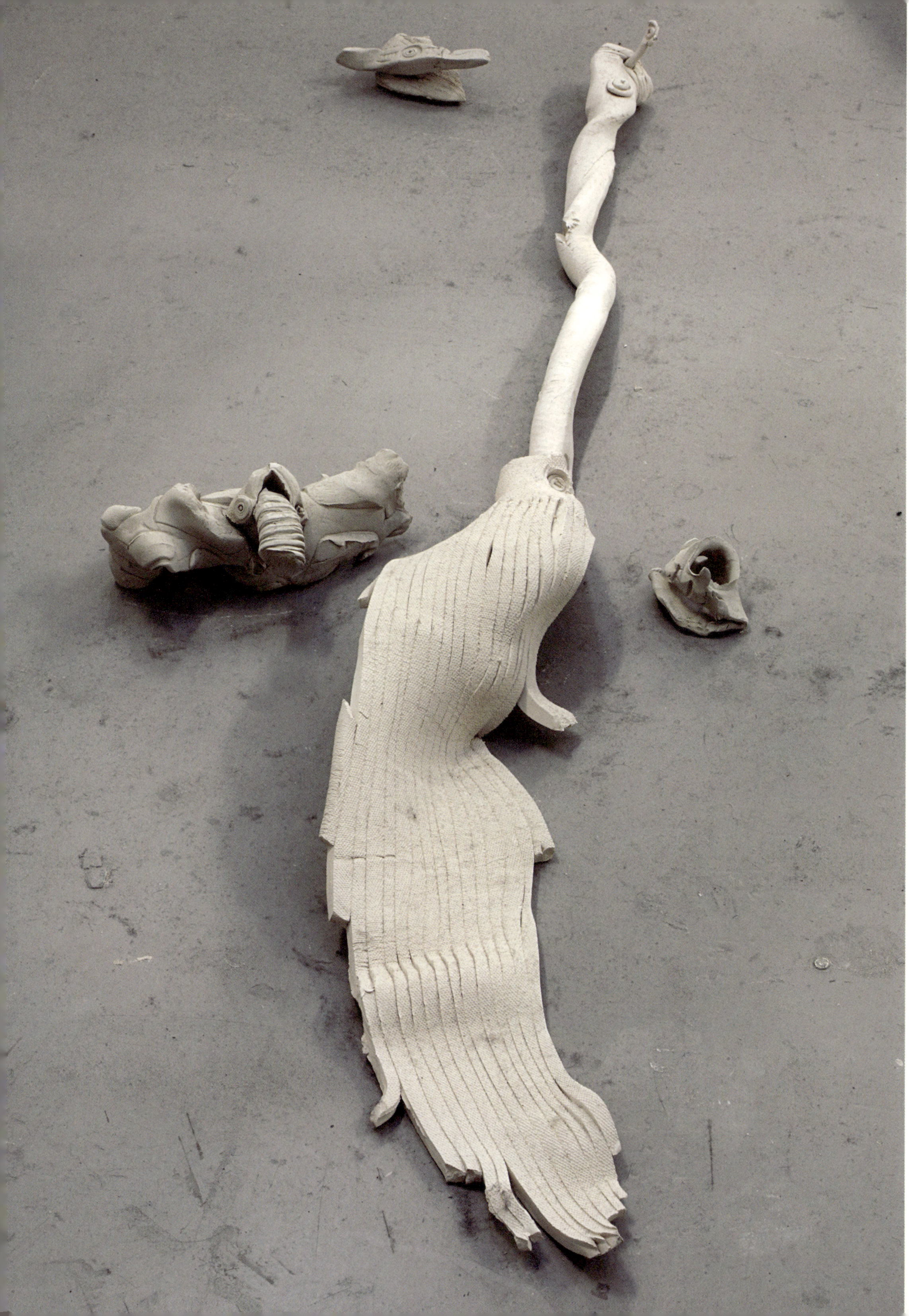

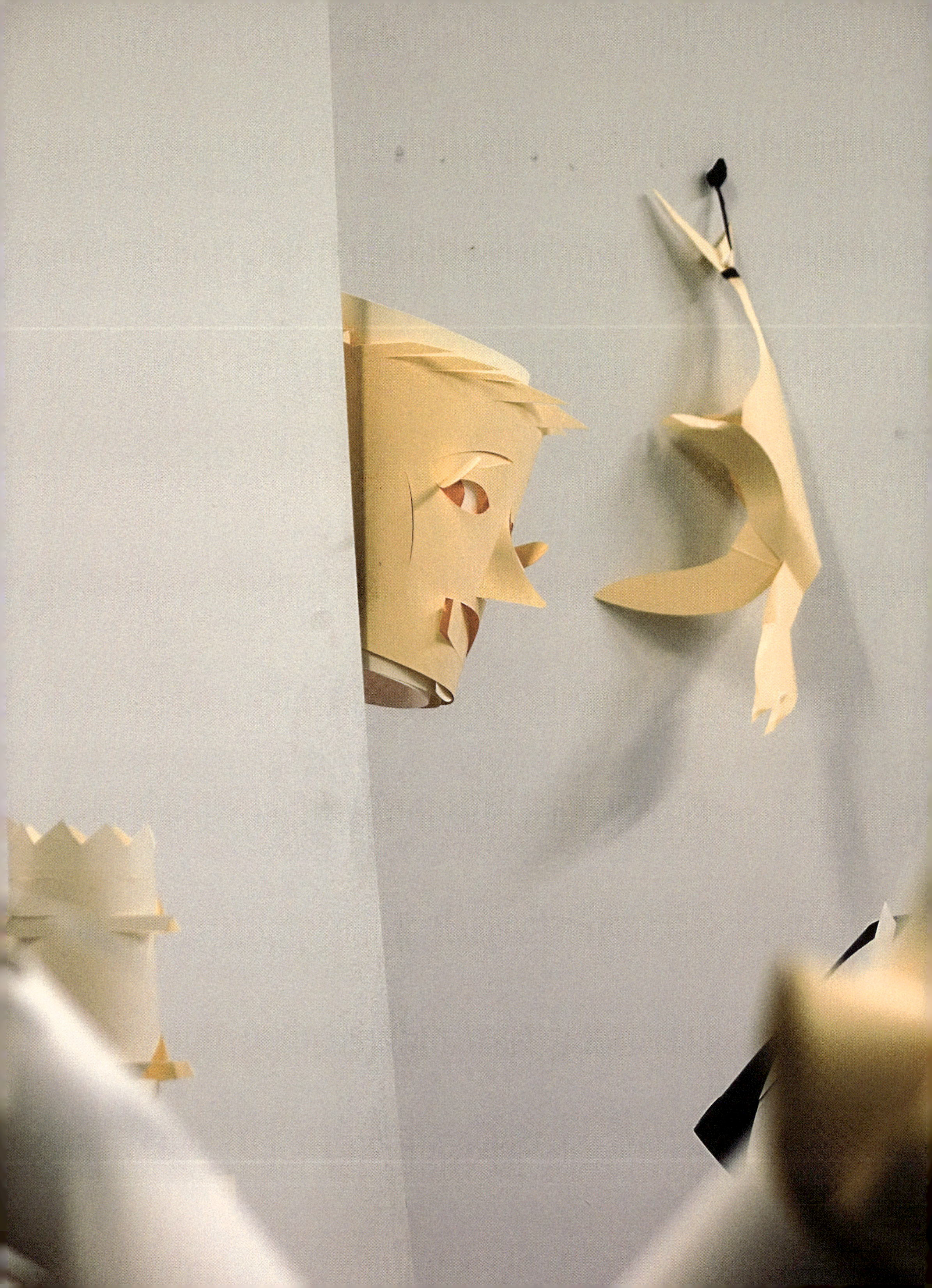

INTRIGE

2006 / INKJET
PRINT ON CANVAS
120 X 140 CM

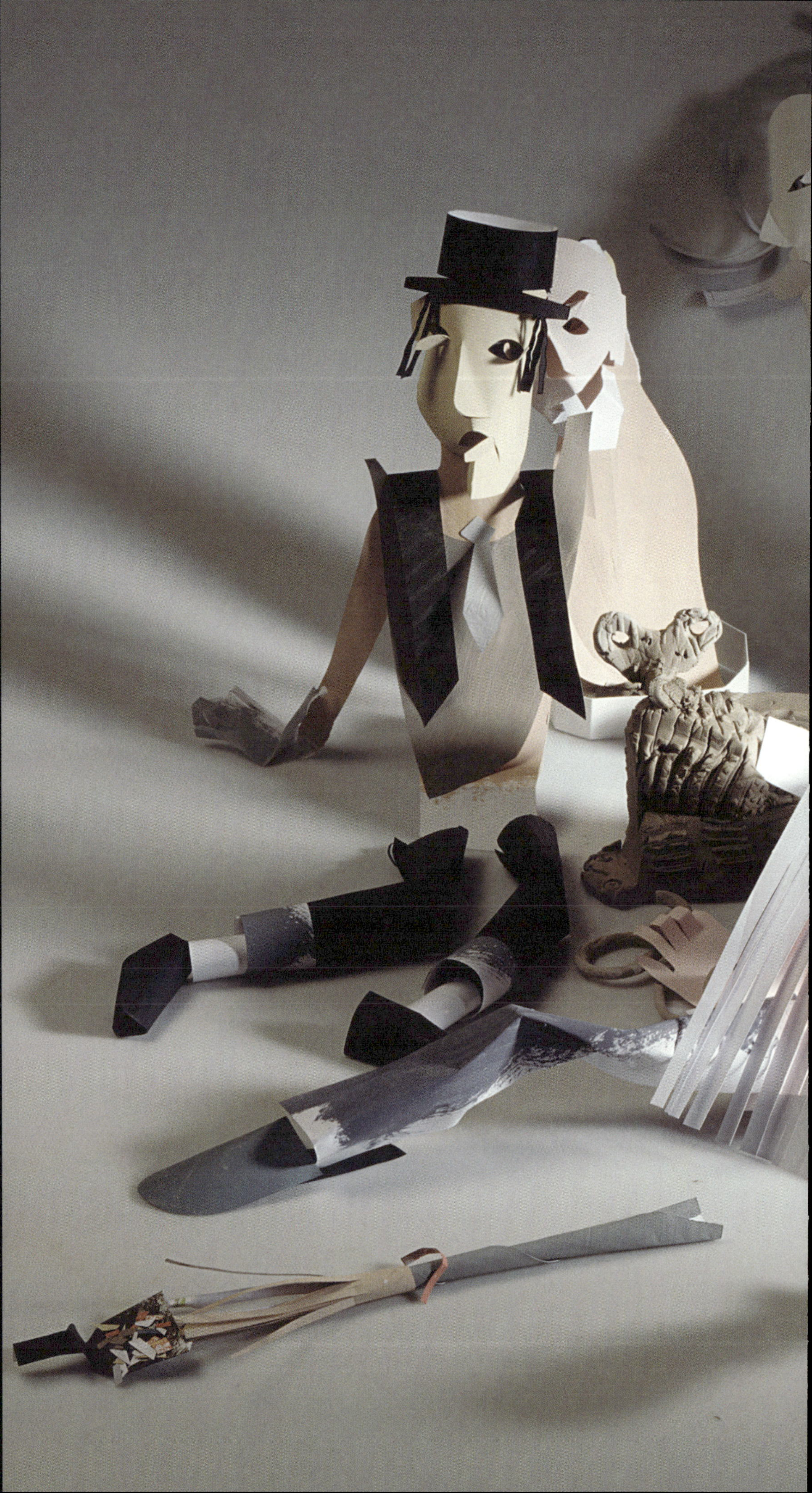

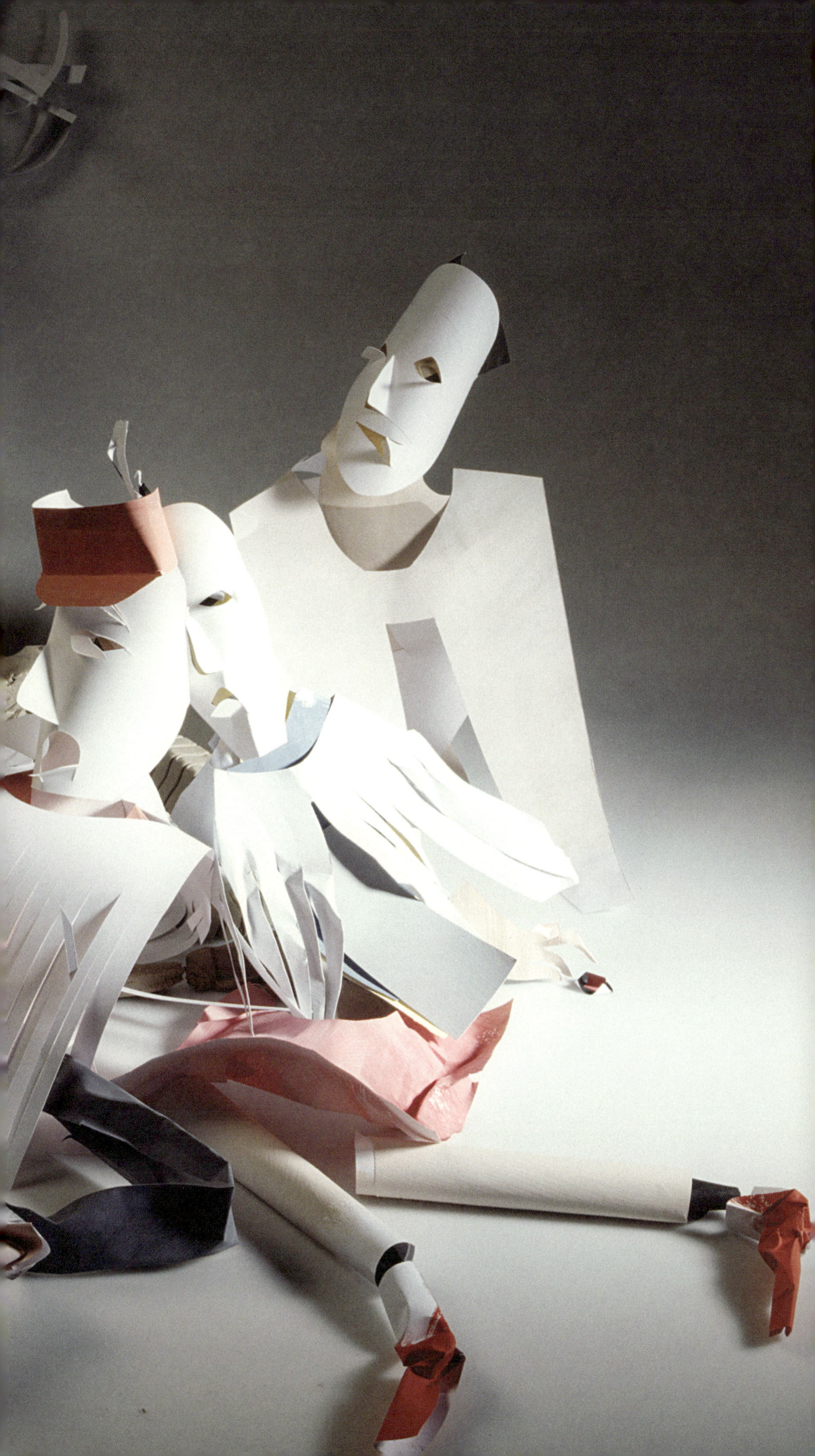

OPERA

2006 / INKJET PRINT ON CANVAS
315 X 245 CM

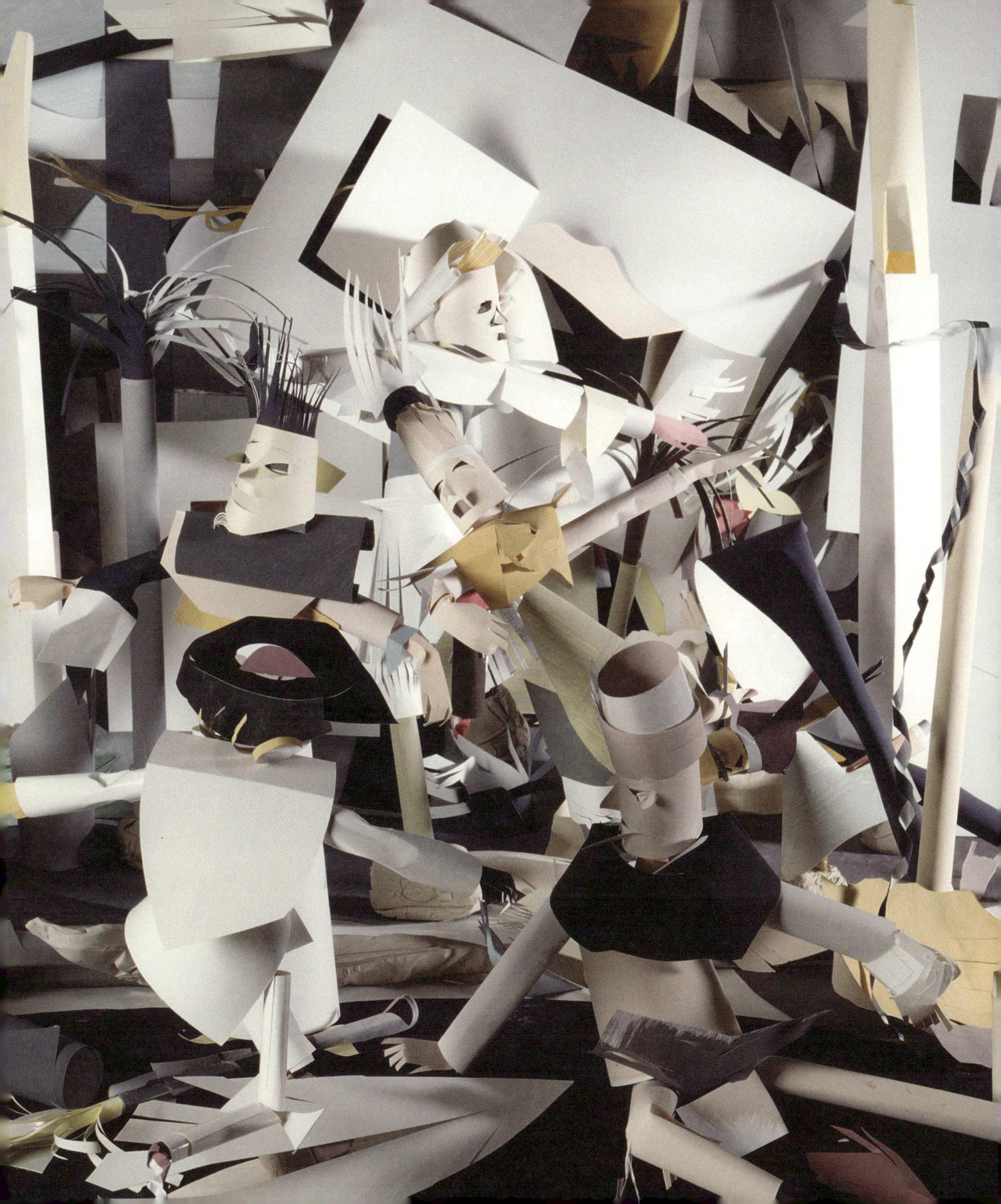

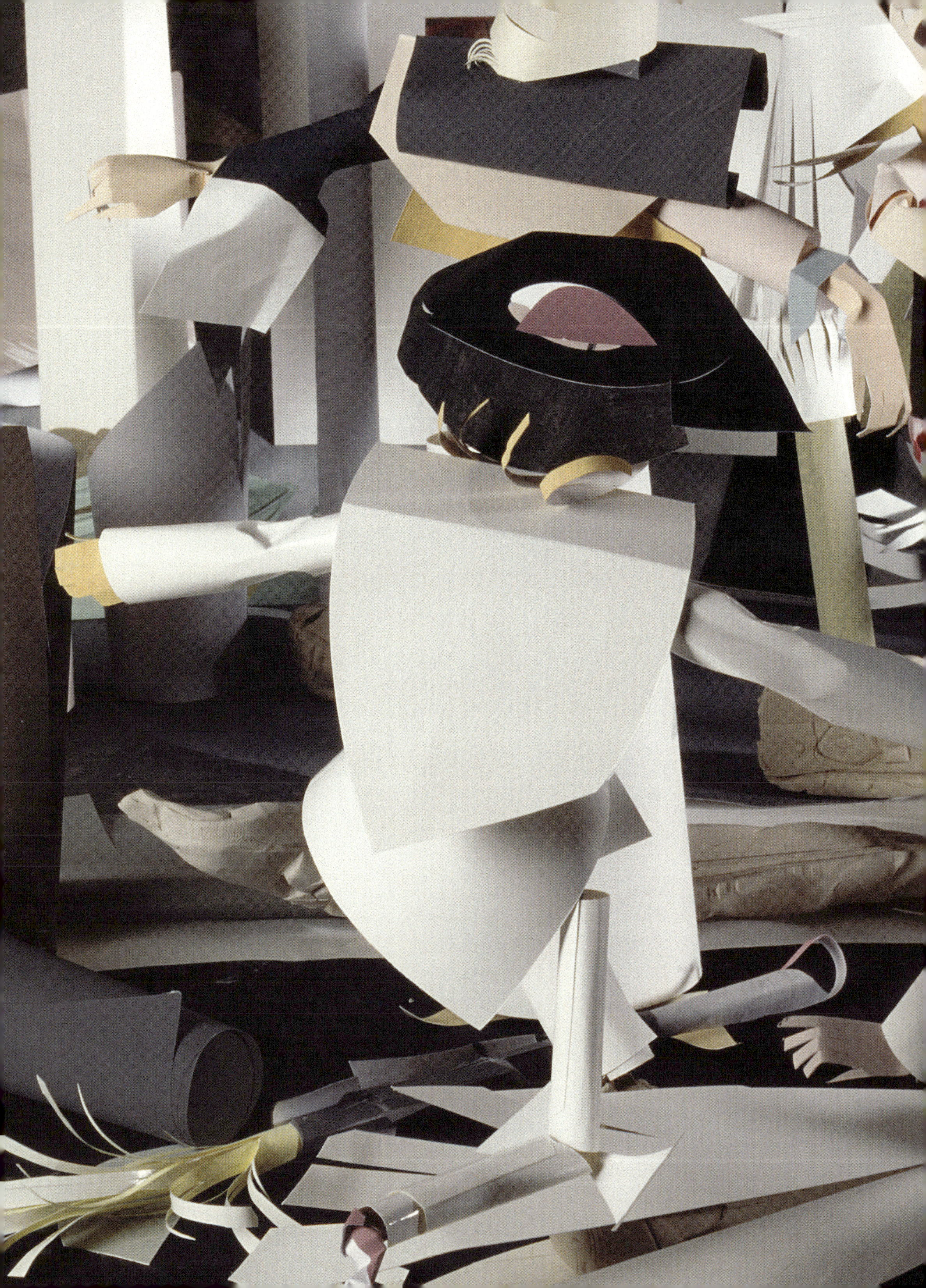

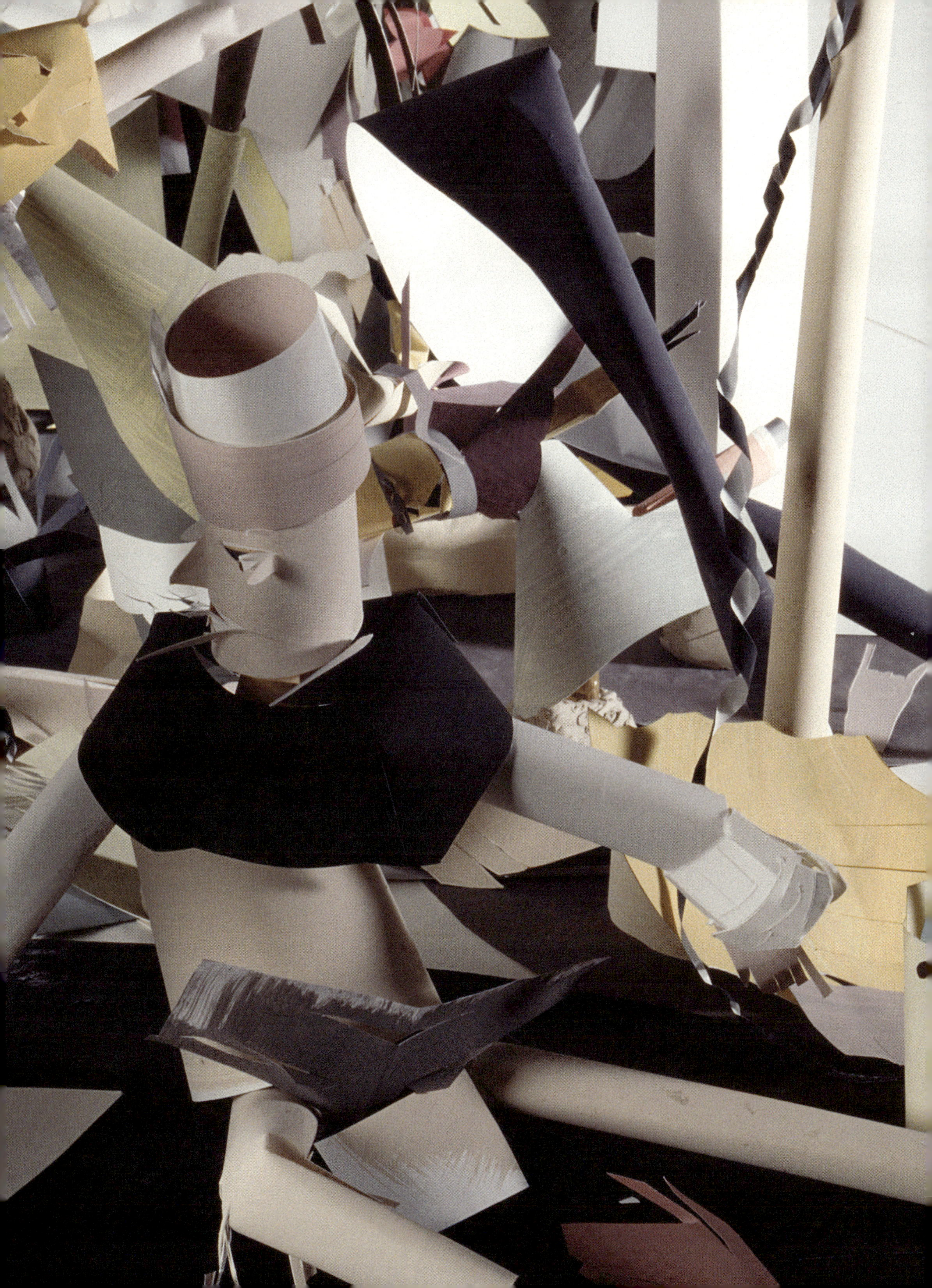

REHEARSAL

2006 / INKJET PRINT ON CANVAS
240 X 310 CM

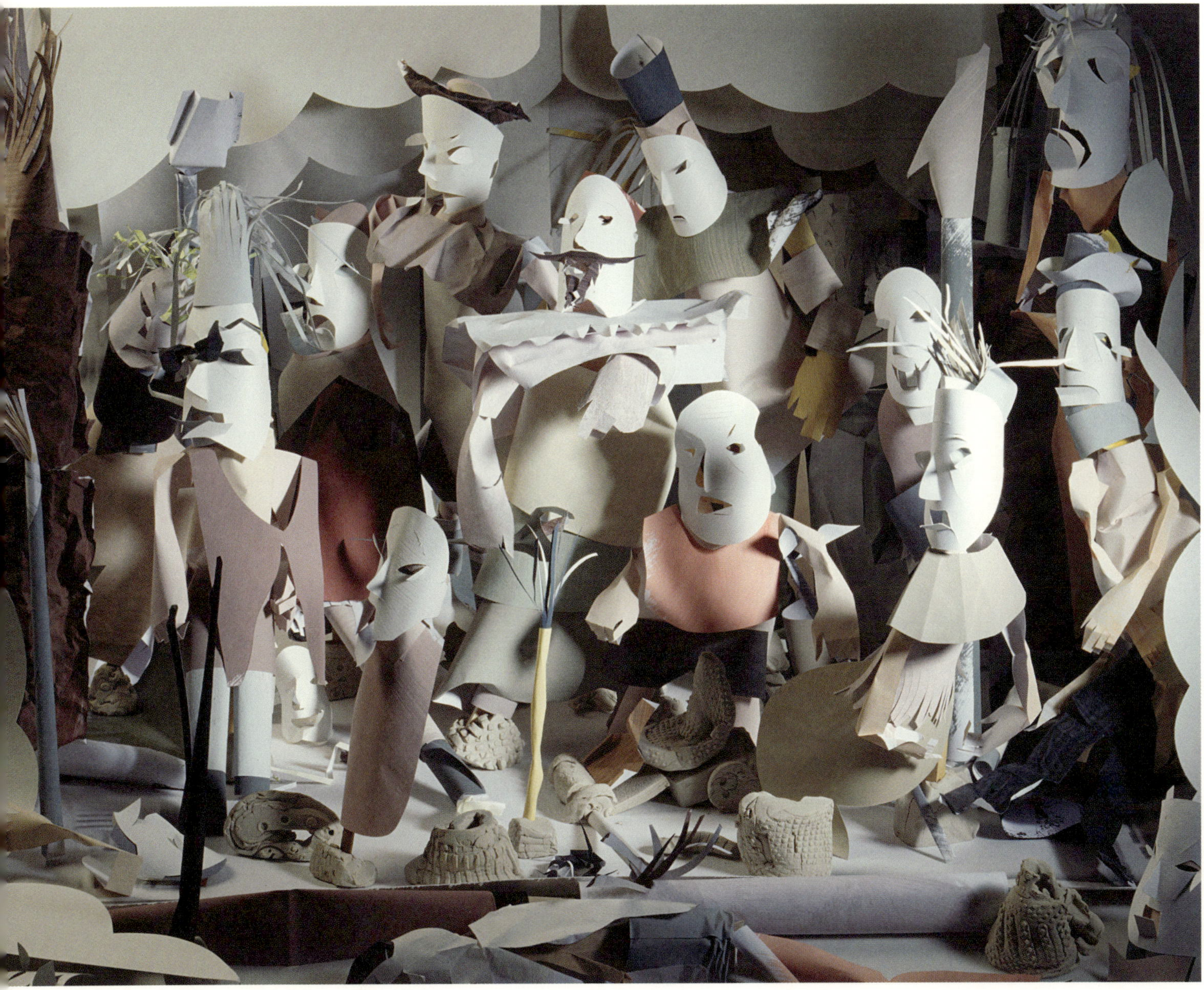

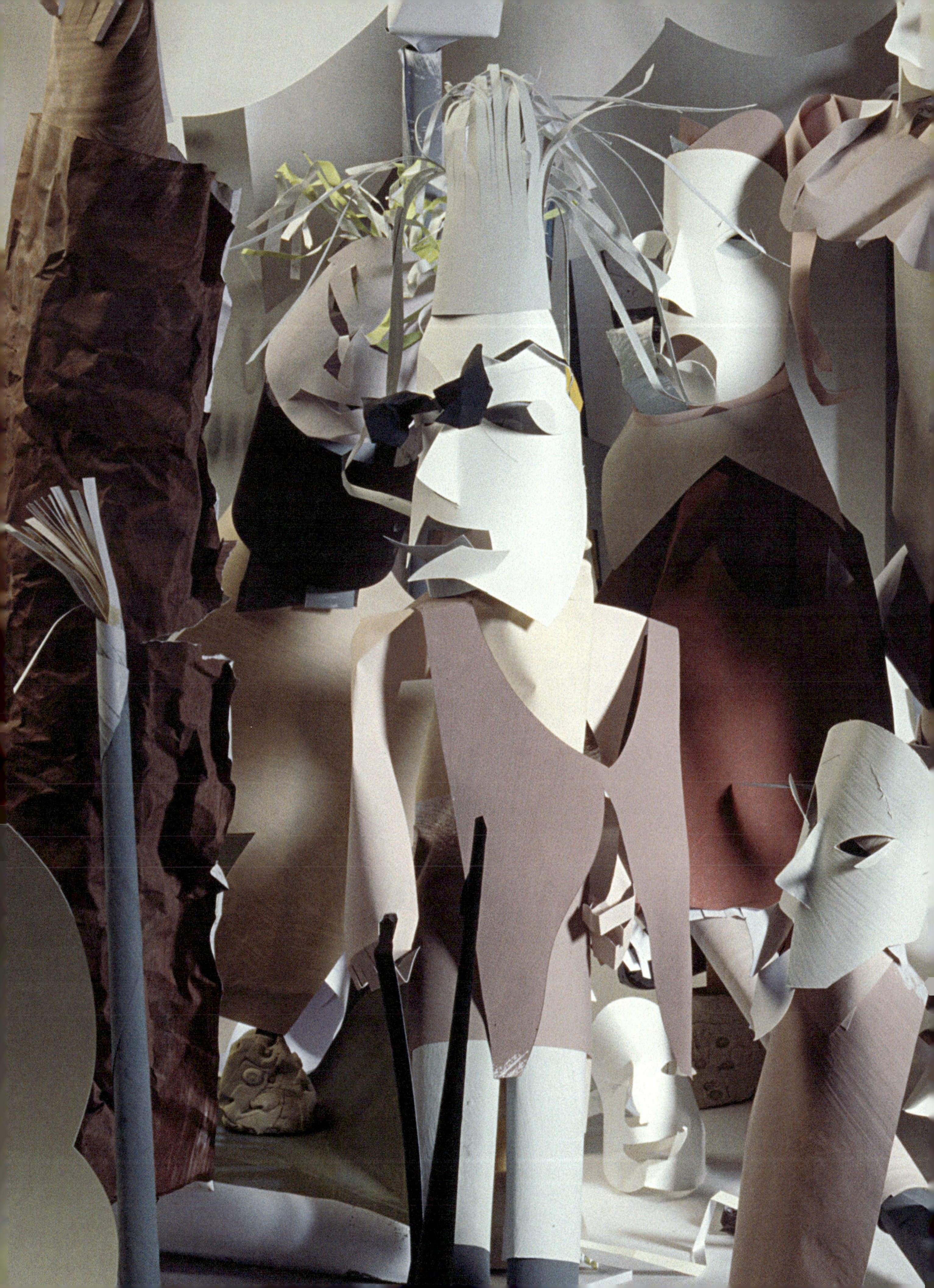

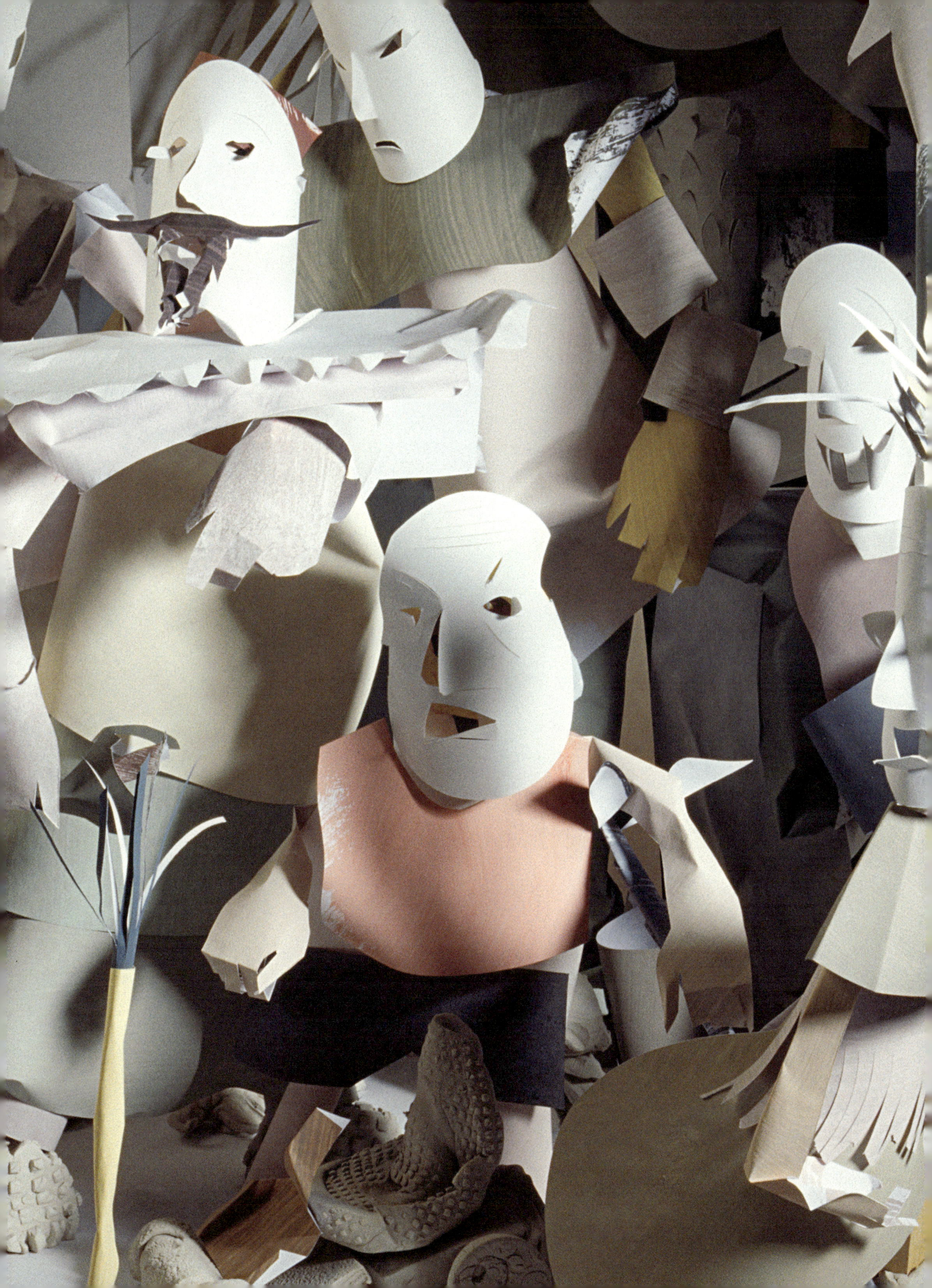

KAREN SARGSYAN
THE TOUCHING

This publication was made possible by Thieme Art, part of Thieme GrafiMedia Groep

Karen Sargsyan is represented by
Galerie Juliètte Jongma
Gerard Doustraat 128A
1073 VX Amsterdam
The Netherlands
Tel & fax 0031 (0)20 463 69 04
info@juliettejongma.com
www.juliettejongma.com

Concept and design Stèphanie de Vilder
Author Ingrid Commandeur
Photography Ilya Rabinovich, Willem Vermaase
Lithography and printing Thieme Amsterdam
Paper Munken Polar, Grafisch Papier, Andelst
Binding Callenbach van Wijk, Utrecht

Acknowledgements
AMC Amsterdam
Amex Collection
Art Amsterdam
Bonnefanten museum
Marc Foxx
Gemak, Den Haag
Hudson Valley Center for Contemporary art, Peekskill, USA
Kunstbeeld
Metropolis M
Bob van Orsouw
Rijksakademie Amsterdam
Villa Romana, Florence, IT
Nicolas Schafhausen
Diana Stigter
Collection Marc en Livia Straus, USA
Thieme Amsterdam
Zonnebanen

Special thanks to
Korjun Sargsyan, Lusi Sargsyan, Mane Sargsyan, Liesbeth Brandt Corstius, Donara Vasilian

Publisher Thieme Art, Deventer
For more information about Thieme Art www.thiemeart.com

ISBN 978 90 789 6415 5
NUR 646

ART
A08
DAM

Thieme Art
Thieme GrafiMedia Groep

FSC
Mixed Sources
Product group from well-managed forests, controlled sources and recycled wood or fiber
www.fsc.org Cert no. CU-COC-802731